MISSIONS

IS A CONTACT SPORT

by

Richard P. Reichert

ISBN: 0-75962-935-8

This book is printed on acid free paper.

1stbooks rev. 10/25/01

DEDICATED TO A DAD who let his teenage son drive five thousand miles on a motorcycle for a short-term missions trip. As with many short-term "ministry" experiences there was more “motorcycle” than "ministry", which, of course, Dad knew all along, but had the good sense to say nothing, because he also knew there would be just enough "ministry" to whet my appetite for more.

CONTENTS

FOUNDATIONS

APPLICATIONS

GETTING STARTED

ACKNOWLEDGMENTS

DAVID NORD is an art teacher at the Alliance Academy in Quito, Ecuador. His technical prowess is under the Lordship of Christ and his art is an extension of his relationship to the Lord. David's students are using murals as a ministry to Ecuadorian society and many of the drab walls of Quito, and beyond, are targets of his Christian Service Outreach group. Several spaces have already been transformed into Christian messages of light and hope. When David is not drawing, he is biking about the country, a laboratory of cross- cultural collisions in itself.

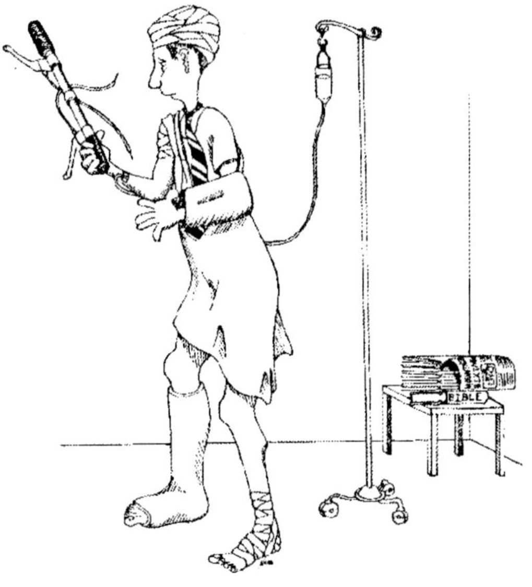

To David goes my gratitude for the cover design and the vast majority of illustrations in these pages. His sensitivity to the subject of cross-cultural contact is evident in every drawing. These are not just cartoons. They are statements that are an integral part of the message of this book. I hope you enjoy them as I did.

To Greg Collord, Larry Thorson, Connie Smith, Paul Johnson, and my wife Hope, colleagues in the trenches of trans-cultural engagement, goes my enormous gratitude for their conscientious evaluation of this manuscript. My son Paul debuts as an artist on page 27.

WHAT THE BOOK IS ABOUT

CONTACT IS THE OPERATIVE WORD in missions today. Everybody wants a hands-on experience. The trend toward short-term assignments and work team projects approaches an epidemic. The market is flooded with tour and team opportunities. The task of managing this vast new missions resource will be huge. This book hopes to be a help. It is written for those who will not be satisfied with less than a personal cross-cultural contact.

Pioneer missionaries of the past, intent on opening new areas for ministry, spoke of "contact" in hushed tones. For them, "contact" meant that first tentative brush with a stone-age tribe or headhunting people. The risk of making contact was often high. Today while contact with other cultures may be more controlled, risk remains. One cannot have significant contact with another race or people without risking who you are, what you have, where you come from, and what you have always understood to be right or even true. This book addresses those who are ready to risk themselves to that degree in order to make significant contact with a second culture.

The title is deliberate. Growing up in the sixties in small-town Western Canada basketball was the new sport on the block. In contrast to the hallowed game of hockey, it was considered a non-contact sport. Later in life I came to realize that basketball as well, while not considered a contact sport, can be a rather physical affair. There is something appealing about human bodies, thrust together on a confined court or ice surface, hurtling about each other. While contact may be more incidental in some sports, it is part of the drama that the closer the bodies come to collision, the more inviting the spectacle.

As with contact sports, when it comes to cross-cultural exposure, seeing how close you can come makes it all the more meaningful, and fun. Missions is clearly a contact sport. Multicultural ministry will always be an abrasive experience, when the rough edges of one culture come in touch with the sharp differences of another. Sometimes the contact is deliberate and direct. At other times, contact with another culture can produce incidental conflict. I was first drawn to the title idea when I read somewhere that "politics is a contact sport." I do not mean to imply with that missions is dirty business. But to properly connect with another culture it is indispensable that you dirty your hands in a different sense. This book deals with how you can do that, and survive.

There are two main thrusts. The early section illustrates from the author's personal experience in a second culture some of the bruises you can expect if you care to make meaningful contact with another people. The later section attempts to show how you can avoid major collisions while still enjoying significant cross-cultural contact.

The purpose of the book is to provide an orientation manual on multicultural awareness. You do not need to be contemplating short-term missions to benefit from the book. But the book is especially aimed at people who are anticipating Christian ministry in another culture. It is written with the short-term missionary in mind, or for anyone who ever had an inkling he might like to be one. The goal is to help those people get the maximum impact out of a short-term contact. And it is published with the prayer that it may be the motivating tool in moving many people out of comfortable mono-cultural living into the exciting arena of cross-cultural ministry, where the risks are only exceeded by the rewards.

TIMBUKTU
WANTED:
SHORT-
TERM
WORKERS

Chapter 1

COMMON MARKS OF A FIRST-TERM MISSIONARY

MOSES WAS NO MARVEL as a cross-cultural communicator. His early experience in ministry demonstrates the classic pitfalls open to a person engaging a second culture for the first time. In his initial attempt at liberating his people he committed some of the common mistakes of a first-term missionary. That is why he makes an excellent case study for anyone anticipating cross-cultural service.

I attended a language school where the program of study was one year in duration. An assortment of missionary hopefuls from a menagerie of missions, fresh from teary home church send-offs, stepped off the plane and into "the culture." There was more new shoe leather on the streets of that city than you see on an average weekend in June in Niagara Falls. Here they were, eager to encounter the culture and learn the language. Most of them had just stepped off the commissioning platform where they were the stars, and onto the plane. Now they were nothing more than a fresh batch of recruits. The language school faculty made it their personal mission to break in each new crop of candidates to the subtleties of the Spanish language and the idiosyncrasies of Latin American culture within the prescribed year. Those who could not be broken in could usually be broken down.

The euphoria of "learning the language" was short-lived. Rote was in.

"Why you say it that way" was not important. There were isolated attempts to bring individual language instructors up to speed in North American pedagogy but soon very few of us bothered to use the "why" word. The institution had relied on raw missionary motivation to keep the majority of its customers on track, and there was no reason to change now. By the second trimester there were occasional visits to the school administration by the linguistically more versatile and volatile types. But the director had seen the breed before, and he could not be budged.

He had heard the complaints about unrealistic assignments, rigid teaching styles, and culturally insensitive or offensive teachers. He would not be intimidated by another crop of inductees. The impatience was predictable. We had come to learn the language as fast as possible, and could have done it faster, if only the culture had not kept getting in the way. By late second trimester there were a number of first-term missionaries who had learned just enough Spanish to be downright dangerous.

The director dug in when committees of student delegates asked for an audience. He knew that if he could survive the second trimester he would withstand the assault. After all, none of his problems ever lasted more than a year. By the beginning of third trimester, the groundswell of grassroots criticism against the institution was usually at its peak. The odd independent missionary was daring to come late to class, to skip a class, or to blatantly disregard a certain tutor.

But most chose to let their manners, or memories of Cross-Culture 101, be their guide. Besides, rumors of outright revolt were being dampened now by visits to the consulates of the country of assignment. Talk turned to "getting out of here" and on to "our country," that glorious goal of our missionary dreams, where it would all be better again. And the director smiled, and counted the applications for next year's class.

As the language director's actions suggest, the first-term missionary is quite predictable. That is perhaps why mission administrators, and veteran missionaries, tend to treat the phenomenon in much the same way. "This too will pass" seems to be the best way to deal with the disease of the first-termer. "They'll get over it," field executives nod understandingly when new recruits request reconsideration of a policy or reevaluation of a strategy.

While the exuberance of short-term workers can be treated with a similar nonchalance, the short-termer, or first-termer brings a vibrancy and sense of immediacy to the scene that is refreshing and useful. Despite his predictability, the first-timer brings some valuable tools to the table that one could hope to see in more veterans. There is something infectious about the open-mouthed awe of a work team on the ride in from the airport. Every time I accompany a new visiting work group or short-term candidate into the field for the first time I think of Moses.

For me, Moses is a prototype of every first-timer engaging in cross-cultural contact. He demonstrates several of the common marks of most first-term missionaries and short-term workers. Often, like Moses, they expect too much, they act too quickly, and they quit too soon.

Moses Expected Too Much

Moses saw himself as a sure bet for success. After all, he had the language, he knew the culture (or he thought he did), and he was well prepared.

But for all his noble aspirations and natural abilities, Moses' naive approach spelled failure. He accomplished nothing. Moses came on strong because he felt he had a lot to offer. "*Moses was educated in all the wisdom of the Egyptians and was powerful in speech and action.*"(Acts 7:22) Who better to help his people than someone with a feel for the palace? His political savvy would be the salvation of his people. So Moses stepped into the situation with both feet.

As a first-term cross-cultural minister I was often surprised that I was so ineffective. One trip to Buena Esperanza was more than enough to deflate the exaggerated expectations I carried into that first term. It was the hometown of a national coworker, little more than a crook in a creek bed with a couple of houses tucked in the notch of a mountain.

We went more out of a sense of duty to my partner, than of devotion to the task. The road was impassable half of the year. The rest of the time it was just plain impossible. Heavy mule traffic during the impassable season worked the slumping slopes to a precarious incline in the direction of the gorge. Our vehicle leaned precariously toward the abyss, and the cutbacks were so sharp the back tire often dangled over the edge.

During the *impossible* stage, hoof traffic ground the trail to a choking red powder. If you opened the window you gagged. If you kept it closed the dust sifted through the floorboards leaving the distinct impression of sitting inside a vacuum cleaner. During the *impassable* season rain transformed the dust into greasy mud.

Like Moses I often misjudged my own coping capabilities. The trip was duly scheduled on our provincial itinerary. The telegram was mailed informing the region of our intended visit. The truck was treated to a day in the mechanic shop. And, because it was a visit back "home", the family of our worker also came along. That meant Rebecca, his five-year-old daughter, was on board. It also meant that because there were not enough plastic bags on board, Rebecca predictably got sick all over the truck. Dust-caked and saddle sore from the five-hour Andes roller coaster, we pulled the truck up in front of an adobe home in Buena Esperanza by early afternoon.

Then it happened, smack in the middle of the marathon of hello handshakes: *Avanzando a pasear*, someone said, in the unique vernacular of those parts. Which being interpreted means, "Just out for a drive, are you?" Then a second, and a third offered the same greeting: "Just out for a drive?" It was like a plague. As if this was the way to greet someone who had pencilled you into his calendar three months before, made a special trip downtown to inform you by telegram a week in advance, and put the truck in the shop for a whole day. And put up with the road, the dust, the doggy bags, and the heat, only to be greeted with the cheerful words, "So you're just out for a drive." As if I would ever come here for anything short of the Great Commission!

For two or three hours we sat on the wood benches on the porch while word went up and down the valley that the "brothers" had come. Slowly the men trickled in as day closed on the valley. Each in turn, as he tied up his mule or stored his machete in the rafters, walked over with a grin and a greeting. *Avanzando a pasear?*

They had heard we were coming. Why weren't they here? The men were in the hills clearing land, hoeing corn, gone to buy a cow in Lauro Guerrero, or selling produce in Macará. After complaining for months that we hadn't visited they weren't even on hand to receive us. And worse yet, they thought I was just out for a joy ride. Didn't they understand what I went through to get here?

Was I really expecting too much? After all, here I was, the bright star of Alliance missions, graduate-schooled in cultural anthropology and missions, seasoned in not two but four years of a home service pastorate, plus a full year of language school training with some free cross-culture communication classes thrown in. Here I was, beating it over this excuse of a road, with my kids up in some missionary boarding school and my wife eight months pregnant back in Loja. And they had the nerve to suggest I might be out for a joy ride. If they only knew what my idea of recreation was.

It was only much later that I learned an enlightening tidbit. In the minds of the locals there were only two categories of vehicle travel: cargo and recreational. No trucks ever came up that road empty. Vehicles were magic mules that made the trip to Buena Esperanza only for profit, only with their truck beds bulging. Since the missionary truck came in lightly loaded it was clearly a case of the second category: recreational. He was *avanzando a pasear*. Thus the men would stay in the fields to do what men do: work.

I know how Moses felt. Schooled in the best Egyptian institutions, he had drawers full of diplomas to demonstrate his preparedness to lead a superpower. He didn't need to be out in the brickyard trying to settle a squabble between sweaty slaves. But somehow he went, expecting that he would instantly be identified as the great savior of his people. And no doubt someone had the nerve to suggest, "Look, it's Prince Moses out for a stroll." I know how Moses felt.

Many times, in my first term of cross-cultural ministry, I expected too much. I expected more speaking and teaching opportunities. I had a barrelful of sermons ready to be translated. Despite the fact that the city church was without a pastor, I was invited into the pulpit only three times in three years. Our expert in rural open-air evangelism never entrusted the microphone into my hands for anything approaching a message. Once he asked me to give my testimony. . . in about the same tone as a circus ringmaster points to the far ring where a rookie clown is holding forth till the tent fills up.

I expected to organize more churches, to see more groups get off the ground, to see more converts, and to build a discipleship group. I expected more direction from my field administration in how to do missionary work, and less interference in my life through tedious language study programs and endless reports. I expected to do better in the language and cope faster with the culture. I expected to be accepted more quickly by the local congregation and welcomed more warmly by the national church. I expected to be consulted and was not. I expected to be encouraged and was not. I expected to be guided and was not.

For anyone aiming at cross-cultural ministry, long or short term, it is a wise exercise to write a full set of expectations, then burn them. Don't enter a cross-cultural challenge with major expectations of success. We come into any cross-cultural context, for all of our brightness and readiness, with the odds weighted against us. We enter that other world primed to conquer, often uninvited, and usually unprepared. Just prying our way into partial acceptance will be a resounding victory. Expectations should be pared to square with that reality.

Moses Acted Too Quickly

Not only did Moses expect too much, he acted too quickly. It is the second fatal trap of all enterprising cross-cultural conquerors. The audacity to cross ethnocultural lines and actually aspire to be a change agent boggles the mind. But that is precisely what a missionary does by definition. That being the case we had better go about the task rather humbly, rather quietly, rather cautiously. Moses did not.

Moses' noble aims were thwarted by a very naive approach. He went off half-cocked. It was a reflex action, not an action arising out of reflection. The Bible account is almost matter-of-fact in the way Moses approached a cross-cultural intervention that he was sadly unprepared for. *"When Moses was forty years old,"* it says, *"he decided to visit his fellow Israelites."* But Moses misread the situation. His mistake was common enough: He attacked a symptom instead of the system.

Some of us will sacrifice anything on the altars of organization, of punctuality, or of supposed principle. We come into a local church and see that the music is a mess, the order of service is all wrong, the worship team needs work, or the ushers are out of step. So we make an initial assessment, go home and pray about it, and come back the next day to tell the national pastor what is wrong with his church.

The danger of acting too quickly is that, while the odds are weighted against success, many people have been conditioned to defer to the foreigner, or at least give lip service to his ideas. We may be initially impressed with how quickly people are "catching on" to our ideas. What in fact is happening is that our tendency to call for minor changes, prematurely, will have a reasonable degree of initial success as long as we do not dabble with larger solutions. If we are not patient enough to wait till we have earned the right to press for larger purposes, we will discover that we have only managed to insulate others from being open to significant change, or have immunized key people from seeing us as serious spokesmen for change.

Moses assumed that liberation from Egypt meant dealing drastically with the Egyptians. He sized up the situation and decided to act. *"He saw one of them being mistreated by an Egyptian, so he went to his defense and avenged him by killing the Egyptian."*

Here we come to the crux of the passage. Good intentions do not count when it comes to cross-cultural communication. Moses' noble ambitions were not well received. *"Moses thought that his own people would realize that God was using him to rescue them, but they did not."*

That text could be the epitaph of many a missionary's career. How often as a first-term cross-cultural minister I assumed I was being received as God's answer to man's need. After all, here I was, a seminary trained, home service honed product of a severe selection process. Through a battery of aptitude tests I had been declared psychologically and linguistically fit to move mountains. I had three children, two master's degrees, one wife, and just enough Spanish to be dangerous.

I had been conditioned by twenty years of denominational missionary conventions and was beginning to believe what I had heard since childhood: "*Our missionaries are the cream of the crop.*" Now selected to that hallowed group, solemnly commissioned, outfitted to the technological teeth, could there be any doubt that I would be royally received?

There must have been a mistake. Moses *thought* that he would be received as a savior, a liberator, a hero, and he was not. He was sure he had something to offer. He came from a broader cultural circle. His familiarity with palace politics, his contacts in the civil service, his pipeline to the budget, all of the advantages of his upbringing, must surely have weighed in his favor. He had so much to offer over any other leader who might emerge from among the smaller circle of Hebrew brick makers. His world was so much more ample, so much more informed. It was an insult not to be instantly recognized as the national solution to his people's plight. There was the issue. They were not "his people," they were "God's people," and the circle of divine cultural awareness was infinitely bigger than even Moses' ample mind set.

Moses' impulsiveness was prompted by that oversight. Tradition tells of a white man who stood on a beach before a simple indigenous man. The white man inscribed a small circle in the sand with a stick, and pointing to it, pronounced, "This is what the Indian knows." Then, tracing a much larger circle that swallowed the small circle, he added, "And this is what the white man knows." The Indian appeared overwhelmed by the prospect. He stood speechless for several seconds, then took the stick in his hand and began to walk off an enormous circle in the sand that dwarfed both circles by its size. When he had closed the circle, he tapped the sand and spoke softly. "This," he said, indicating the third circle, "This is where the Indian and the white man know nothing."

Moses' circle was big in terms of the provincial world of his fellow Hebrews and what he had to offer them. But in terms of what God had in mind for His people, Moses' skill and training meant nothing. Moses wanted to be their leader. God wanted to lead them out. Deliverance from the Egyptians meant deliverance from Egypt. Moses' idea of liberation was too narrow for what God wanted to do. It was clear that Moses would have spent the rest of his life patching up injustices and putting bandages on the social abuses against his people. Killing the Egyptians off, one at a time, would have been a slow way to set his people free. When Jehovah God got around to settling scores at the Red Sea, He did it much more effectively, and much more efficiently.

Moses' second attempt at arbitration was an even more abysmal failure. This time he set out to settle a score between two fellow Hebrews. He assumed that they saw his role as ruler as clearly as he himself did. Again, sizing up the situation, he acted quickly . . . too quickly. How harsh it is to hear the words, "You don't understand how we think," when we try to intervene between national brothers, only to be brushed aside. I worked with a group of Ecuadorian young people for two and a half years when one of them blurted out one day, "Brother, we are just now starting to trust you." I was crushed. I had felt we had been on the same wave length for over a year, that they listened to me and had accepted me long ago. REMEMBER, you will be held at cultural arm's length for much longer than you think. If, in that undefined period before full acceptance, you open up with both barrels as Moses did, you will effectively short-circuit any ministry among the people you have accepted long before.

Moses' rash intervention immunized an entire generation against accepting him as their liberator. He may have enjoyed the momentary flush of addressing an obvious injustice, but his positive action was viewed as an overreaction. He was categorized as impulsive and was dismissed as a prospective deliverer of his people. Sadly, premature engagement as cultural change agents can do more damage than just sitting and doing nothing. We can commit the cultural equivalent of a "mission miscarriage" faster than we care to admit. We do not earn the right to correct people, especially of another race, or to suggest changes in their way of doing things, easily or quickly.

Moses Quit Too Soon

Not only did Moses expect too much and act too quickly, he fell neatly into that most common of traps for would-be cross-cultural explorers. He quit too soon. Stung by his own failure, Moses threw in the towel. As such he qualifies as a classic first-term dropout. He was overgenerous in his personal assessment of himself. Overzealous, he committed what amounted to cultural overkill, and finally, oversensitive in his response to criticism, he went off to sulk in the desert and to lick the wounds of his deflated ego.

Moses decided that he was not cut out for this missionary thing. He miscalculated the size of the mission. He gave up. Unprepared for criticism, he packed his barrels and headed home. It is scary to see first term colleagues selling all of their things and selling themselves short of success. Incredibly, many short term missions visitors can come to the definitive decision that they are not cut out for cross-cultural ministry in a matter of a few weeks. One college intern made the decision after a single weekend trip to the jungle!

The curious thing about Moses' letter of resignation is that it was written on the run. Acts 7:29 says that "*at this remark Moses fled.*" (Acts 7:29 NASB) It does not say "*at this blow Moses ran for his life*," or even "*at this threat on his life, Moses took off.*" It simply says, "*at this remark*" Moses fled. He ran at the drop of a remark. The old playground taunt, "sticks and stones may break my bones, but words will never hurt me," is a blatant lie. Words usually do hurt us. But words spoken in criticism from across cultural trenches have a devastating effect.

I often wonder what kind of a missionary speaking tour Moses had in the Midian desert. I suspect he dumped a lot of sour grapes on the ungrateful Israelis back in Egypt who had not identified him as their savior. His slide presentations were woefully "first-term". There was little success to report. There were some moral victories but few spiritual victories. He had to content himself with doing a historical cultural presentation because when he was very honest about it all, his first term had been a miserable failure.

In the last year of our first term my wife, Hope, pulled together a very popular charm course for adolescent girls. The effort seemed like too little, too late. With barely months to go in that same term it seemed like my personal dream of forming a significant discipleship group was also doomed. People were just not responding. Much like Moses I tended to sweep all of my shortcomings under the rug of misunderstanding. *"Moses thought that his own people would realize that God was using him to rescue them, but they did not."* Then, when I had given up, the Lord put it all together, and six key young men committed themselves to my group. It was a clear case of too little, too late, or was it?

It has taken the perspective of several years before we can correctly evaluate the results of those two small groups. It was just a pebble tossed in a pond at the end of a very ordinary first term. Yet two of the girls in Hope's little charm class have since gone on to seminary. To this day several of those girls look to her as a model and spiritual advisor.

Fifteen years have passed since my first dismal discipleship group experience. One of those boys is now a pastor. Two others are key lay leaders in the local church. While we live in a distant city, the infrequent contacts with the members of those two insignificant first-term ministries are like family reunions. They call and visit us. We are friends. While we had given up on significant first term ministry, the Lord had not given up on us.

Expecting too much, acting too quickly, quitting too soon: These are the marks of a first-term missionary. Gratefully, God allowed me, as he did Moses, a second chance. But before we can enjoy that glorious page of Moses' ministry it is essential to walk with him through his first furlough. The Midian desert was not Moses' choice for a furlough from cross-cultural ministry. He was on the run, and he ran right into the Lord's training camp. The text says "*When Moses heard this he fled to Midian where he settled as a foreigner and had two sons.*"(Acts 7:29 NIV) There were lessons to be learned: three in drab desert tones, and one in three-dimensional technicolor.

The Feeling of Being a Foreigner

A man like Moses had never known the discomfort of committing a linguistic mistake. First-termer all have their own stories. In Spanish the interchanging of a single vowel can land you in more hot water than you can imagine. For example, *ovejas* means sheep but *abejas* means bees. One missionary called his congregation a bunch of bees during an entire sermon. A colleague was asked the secret of his wife's favorite recipe.

"First of all, she starts with a hot bra," he said with a straight face. He intended to say that you start with a hot frying pan (*sartén*) but used the local word for ladies' lingerie instead (*sostén*).

Feeling like a foreigner is uncomfortable, embarrassing, and at times downright humiliating. Most of the time people put up with the funny way we talk. Yet sometimes at social gatherings they will let down their guard and a *gringo* joke slips out. Because the Latinos I know are so deeply sensitive to offending people they only dare to try a joke at the North American's expense when they are comfortable that they have his confidence. Still, as much as one smiles and tries to be the brave butt of the joke, the feeling of being a foreigner seeps through and you wish you could just fit in without being noticed as different.

For me, the feeling can best be summed up by the "lettuce" joke. More often than not, for want of fresh material to keep the party lively, or when the *tamale* being served recalls the stale story, someone is sure to try it out in your presence once or twice a term. I have heard it so often I can feel it coming.

Right in the middle of a *tamale* or a dry corn cake *humita*, the "lettuce joke" is sure to take shape. Both delicacies are cooked and served in a leaf wrapping that conserves the heat and the flavor. It's up to the guest to open up the leaf and eat what's inside.

"Did you hear about the *gringo* who was served his first *tamale*?" someone ventures. Everyone has heard it, but hearing it again, with a foreigner present who has certainly never heard it, will be fun. No one lets on to having heard the story. The would-be comedian warms to the task and squares himself for the punch line. Some do it better than others. I have heard it enough that I cringe at the crippled attempts to embellish the joke till the point of it is all but lost in the telling. At any rate no one lets on they have ever heard of the North American trying his first *tamale*.

When he was all finished, the host asked: "And how did you enjoy the *tamale*?"

"*Mucho bueno*," the gringo is reported to have said, slaughtering the King's Spanish. "It was very good, but the lettuce was a little tough."

The room breaks out in hilarious delight at the expense of the fictitious foreigner who didn't know enough to eat only the insides, but ate the green leaf wrapping as well. Everyone glances at the gringo to be sure he got the joke, and someone will be kind enough to repeat the punch line a time or two, explaining it as he goes. I must confess that in my more unsanctified moments I have been tempted to preempt the next telling by just grabbing a *tamale* and gobbling the whole thing down, "lettuce" and all, refueling the rumor, and guaranteeing the retelling of the "lettuce joke" on unsuspecting first-termers for another millennium or two!

Nobody likes to be the butt of the "lettuce joke". I'm sure that it was not till he got to the desert that Moses heard his first "Egyptian" joke. The bilingual Moses struggled with a new vocabulary for the first time in his life. He was the outsider at the table. A man who was "*powerful in words*" in another setting was reduced to a stuttering child. But the Lord knew that the man who would lead his people through foreign territory would need to know the feeling of being a foreigner, first. The desert of cross-cultural discomfort can be bleaker than any Sahara. Once the Jews were cut loose from Egypt they would be wandering on strangers' soil without roots for years. It would take a man with tough cultural skin to walk them through that desert.

The Secret of Shepherding

We know that Moses attached himself to a family of shepherds, and that the pride of Egypt's palace with his uncalloused hands and fine upbringing got his first taste of the real world plodding over desert sands looking for places to pasture his sheep. The lessons learned with a staff in his hand and the grit of sand in his sandals were not things you could pick up in the palace. God knew that if Moses was ever to be useful as a liberator he would have to learn how to lead like a shepherd.

The domineering leadership style of the Pharaoh would not work for the job Moses would be called to do. I will never forget the fatherly advice of a district superintendent who reminded me as I moved toward my first pastorate, "Just remember, God has called us to be shepherds, not cowboys." The cowboy drives his livestock, the shepherd leads his flock by going on ahead of them. One tells them where to go, the other shows them how.

The Pharaohs were "cowboy" leaders who whipped people into shape by physical force and intimidation. Moses had to be reprogrammed for shepherding, and there was only one place he could learn it. God knew, too, that if Moses were to spend the rest of his life in a desert, and if he were to lead people through a desert, it would be wise to have some desert mileage on his staff. The staff became Moses' trademark. What to Egyptian minds was a tool of ignorance became God's rod of power and a symbol of divine authority in Moses' hand. There was a time when Moses would not have been caught dead in the palace with a staff in his hand. But after his desert boot camp it appears that he went nowhere without it. It was a symbol of his new leadership style.

God left him in a desert for forty years to learn the secret of shepherding sheep in order to equip him to shepherd the flock of God. It's the same lesson God used to equip David. "*He chose David his servant and took him from the sheep pens; from tending the sheep he brought him to be the shepherd of his people Jacob, of Israel his inheritance. And David shepherded them with integrity of heart and with skillful hands he led them."* (Psalm 78:70,71) Shepherding skills were transferable to managing human resources.

The Challenge of Raising Children

Family life can be an important crucible for refining cross-cultural skills. In Moses' case it's so matter of fact we could miss it all together. "*When Moses heard this, he fled to Midian, where he settled as a foreigner, and had two sons."* Moses must have thought that Midian was where he would settle for the rest of his days. He married a local shepherd gal and they had children. There are lessons learned in the laboratory of a family that cannot be taught in any class. There is something about parenting that prepares you for leadership like no other school. For those who are married, family life can be a litmus test of readiness for cross-cultural encounter. It should never be looked on as an interlude before ministry begins.

Act Three: GOD

If Moses' failed attempt at ministry can be considered Act One of this little drama, and his Midian years of relearning important lessons are Act Two, then one final act remains.

The burning bush is the pivot on which Moses' re-education hinges. What Moses learned in forty years as a foreigner, chasing stray sheep and spanking bratty kids, was essential undergraduate training. What he learned in forty minutes at a burning bush was God's graduate school.

> *"Then the Lord said to him, 'Take off your sandals; the place where you are standing is holy ground. I have indeed seen the oppression of my people in Egypt. I have heard their groaning and have come down to set them free. Now come, I will send you to Egypt.'"*
>
> Acts 7:34

What a difference it makes when God gets involved! There is no doubt that Moses had seen the oppression of his people in Egypt. I am convinced that he had heard their groaning and that his well-intentioned intervention was aimed at setting them free. The only problem is that God was not ready yet. Moses had done it on his own. Now the Lord makes it clear that He is directly involved. "*I have seen . . . I have heard . . . I have come down.*" The initiative is clearly divine. Moses will be a player in the drama but only because the Lord has called him off the bench. "*I will send you. . . !*" If there is a missionary call for Moses, this is it!

Moses' second chance is a dramatic reversal of his first tentative attempt at cross cultural intervention. The change is so dramatic that twice the writer underlines the fact: "*this same Moses*" —who expected too much, who acted too quickly, and who quit too soon— now appears to be a totally different man. The would-be change agent was himself a changed man.

Each time it comes to the author with a renewed sense of surprise. Moses was now missionary material.

"This Moses whom they disowned...God sent." (Acts 7:35). This same Moses who had expected too much of himself and others, God now sends, and Moses never looks back for the approval of anyone else. *"This man led them out . . ."*(Acts 7:36) The one who had come off half-cocked, acting too quickly to accomplish any lasting change, now not only returns to lead them, but comes back to lead them out.

What a difference full deliverance makes! The transformation is staggering. *"This is the Moses who said to the sons of Israel, "God shall raise up a prophet LIKE ME from your brethren."* (Acts 7:37) The same Moses who quit too soon, who ran at the drop of a remark, now speaks with the voice of a prophet. For a fourth and final time the preacher punctuates his message with a demonstrative declaration. "*This is the one . . .*" (Acts 7:38) Here was a man who was in touch with God but with both feet firmly planted on the ground. He not only dealt with the grit of sand in his sandals, and dirtied his day with the complaints of a discontented lot, but "*he received living oracles to pass on to you.*" He wrote for posterity. Here was the man who penned the Pentateuch. He was with men, but so in touch with God that when he left, he left something behind. Moses made his mark. It is the crowning touch on an amazing cross-cultural career.

There are no real "naturals" when it comes to missionary material. There are few first-term giants. Like many of the men of faith, Moses was one of those who "*BECAME mighty in war.*" (Hebrews 11:34) God is in the business of making missionary warriors. He is willing to make you and me fit to fight. As we recognize through the mirror of Moses the characteristics of our unsuccessful first flings at cross-cultural ministry, let us take courage in the God who did not give up on him. Like Moses we can "*become* mighty in war" if we are willing to let God work on us. Take heart! The same Moses who expected too much, who acted too quickly, and who quit too soon was retooled for the task to become the mighty liberator of a captive culture. And He is waiting to do it again, through you.

A FORMULA FOR FIRST-TIME FAILURE

Noble Aspirations + Natural Abilities + Naive Approach = Nothing Accomplished

AN ORIENTATION EXERCISE

To make Moses' experience applicable to your situation:

- ❑ List the expectations you have set for yourself on this first cross cultural encounter. What do you hope to accomplish? Keep the list and review it on the return flight home.
- ❑ Assess the positive natural abilities you bring to the experience. What makes you think you have what it takes to succeed or survive in a cross cultural setting?

Chapter 2

COLLISION OR COLLAPSE

MISSIONS IS A CONTACT SPORT. My teenage daughter's face turned green under her Sunday morning makeup. We had just squeezed into the pew for Sunday School in our downtown Latin-American church. The bench was already occupied by a middle-aged man. "Dad," she gagged, "He just spit on the floor." Regaining her composure she attempted to catch up with the chorus being sung. Later we analyzed the incident.

Spitting in public is not a cultural taboo at lower levels of Latin culture. It is a notch or two up the acceptable conduct ladder from urinating in public. A missionary colleague and I would pass the time driving from one rural appointment to another, awarding spitting style points to some of the country women we knew. It worked something like the scoring of a platform dive: distance as well as degree of difficulty entered into the final tabulation. Difficulty meant accuracy. Hitting a half-open doorway from the middle of the living room without skipping a beat in the Bible study usually caught the eyes of the judges. Style had to do with the general toss of the head, the flair with which anyone launched a wad. A heavy-set mother in Pindal was declared the hands down winner.

Considering the almost cultic quality of sport in North America, my daughter and I believe we may have made a significant anthropological discovery. We observed that American religious rituals also include spitting. American baseball players unleash undetermined gallons of the goop in a single season, and a good amount of it before network cameras. Our unprofessional analysis was that the American baseball player and the

Ecuadorian pew spitter had one thing in common. They both spit on sacred spots. The only real difference being that our athletic spitting rites are aired on national television before millions of sophisticated viewers.

Cross-cultural ministry by its very nature is a contact sport. And the contact is not always pleasant. Whether it's spitting in public or eating chicken with your fingers (highly frowned on in my Latin circles), when two different world views collide there are bound to be bruises. One personal collision comes to mind.

What do you do when a tire repairman melts your tire tube before your very eyes? We had just completed a two week cross cultural communications course in Quito— taught at a graduate level no less. I had earned a B. . . not bad. If ever anyone should be primed to confront the peculiarities of a foreign culture, to understand and to cope with any cross cultural crisis, to smile and instantly identify the clues of intercultural tension when an incompetent kid fries his imported truck tire tube before his very eyes, I was the man.

We were about an hour from home when I saw I was losing air in the back tire and, just in time, spotted a vulcanizing shed at the side of the road. The tell-tale signs of a fully functioning tire shop were there: a steel handled hand-made sledge hammer and a sharpened piece of broken leaf spring, a perfect pry bar. Every respectable tire shop has one or two.

Back in the dark recesses of his establishment were the other two pieces of essential equipment: a hammock, and his single concession to technology: an air compressor. Oh yes, and the inevitable iron. The iron was a clothes iron, vintage 1935, welded onto a vise-like screw-down press. The tube and patch are placed under the iron, and the iron is screwed down onto the patch. I knew I was in a legitimate tire shop because of the iron— no switch needed, just two bare wires, one already in the socket; the other he inserted into the socket with two skillful fingers and I knew I was in good hands.

Finally there was the delicate temperature control that guaranteed the iron would not be applied too long to the patch, causing unpleasant words between the technician and the client. You see, a warning light goes on when the correct temperature has been achieved so that perfect patching is all but guaranteed. There can be no mistakes. The thermostat is very simple: a common match placed on the heating iron in just the right spot will ignite when threshold heat has been achieved. Two deft fingers then remove a single wire from the socket, and presto! The tire is done to a turn.

As he began to clamp the cooker onto my almost new imported Goodyear truck tube, I went back to the truck to assure my wife that we truly were in expert hands.

So what do you do when this clod from another culture cooks your tire before your very eyes? What do you do when your imported Goodyear truck tube is fried right in front of you? What did they teach you in Cross-cultural Communications 504? How do you handle that helpless, hopeless feeling of having been had? Missions is a contact sport.

We react. Sometimes we get caught up in the spirit of our host culture. For instance, I saw a lady scurrying around in the luggage area of the Miami airport. Everyone was grabbing for luggage carts so they could be first in line at customs, and this lady who had been traveling all day in Latin America forgot she was safely at home in her own culture. She was so caught up in the spirit of the thing that she was crashing carts, and racing with her suitcases to get into the next lineup. Then she caught herself and said to her husband, " I feel like I'm in a competition."

Sometimes after four years of being "in a competition" we missionaries have absorbed some of that intensity. Some of that grabbiness. We get caught up unconsciously in the spirit of the culture.

When someone robs your home or commits some other illegal offense against you, the correct procedure in Latin America is to "denounce" the person as they put it. You file a complaint. The police will not act on your behalf unless you are willing to file a complaint, and then usually only half-heartedly when you DO go to the trouble.

A bus driver sideswiped my van mirror, tore the frame right out of the sheet metal sockets, and kept on driving. I stepped on the gas, swerved into his lane, and heard the ugly crunch of what was left of my mirror go under my own tire. But I raced on, and cut the bus off, swerving in front of him so that he was wedged in traffic in the middle of an intersection. I rolled down my window and started to shout at him, to "file my complaint" just as I had seen so many others do. But then as the passengers on the bus started to boo me, I realized sheepishly that I had been drawn into the mood of the moment. While hit and run is illegal anywhere, my reaction had gone over a subtle boundary that delineates how a foreigner acts in a host culture.

Because cross-cultural ministry is a contact sport we have often groped for an explanation to the hurt or wonder we experience at having been offended by the other culture. We sometimes call it culture shock.

CULTURE SHOCK is supposedly that moment when my culture collides with another. David Pollock put it most succinctly when he said "the biggest shock is discovering that wherever you go, there you are." Stephen Donaldson in *LORD FOUL'S BANE* suggests two ways by which a man can deal with culture shock.

> *"Culture shock is what happens when you take a man out of his own world and put him down in a place where the assumptions—the standards of being a person—are so different that he can't possibly understand them. He isn't built that way. If he's—facile—he can pretend to be someone else until he gets back to his own world. Or he can just collapse and let himself be rebuilt—however. There's no other way."*[1]

There is more than a little wisdom in those words. To my way of seeing things, "culture shock" is a gross misnomer. It is the extreme case of an individual who has been unable to cope with another culture. Most of us live in the gray fog of cultural fatigue. We adapt, adjust, and cope until, like the strut of an aircraft under constant strain, we give out, not in some catastrophic basket-case collapse, but in a gradual burn-out in which we just can't bear to face the foreignness of things any longer.

Missions is definitely a contact sport. The options open to anyone wishing to engage another culture are not all that exciting. They amount to two: Give up or give in.

Each of us has an undetermined tolerance threshold beyond which we refuse to be rebuilt. Sooner or later in your experience with a second culture you will say, "I've gone far enough. I've been flexible, adapted to their ways, eaten their food, let them poke into my privacy, but this is too much."

The honeymoon experience of first-termers or short-termers is common. They love everything and everyone, for a while. What is probably happening is that they are operating in a glass cocoon of cultural acceptance. They are not really relating to the culture in a realistic way, but have agreed to give up their normal way of reacting to people or things. They are pretending to be someone else. Sooner or later that bubble of unnatural tolerance is destined to burst. Unfortunately, many people who do short term cross-cultural assignments never stay long enough for the bubble to burst. They go home on a false high. "It was great!" They're the friendliest people I've ever met. It's the most beautiful place in the world." Then when career missionary Jones comes calling during his furlough year, the home church folks can't understand his gripes about punctuality, dishonesty or laziness.

People who have insulated themselves from culture shock will not easily understand the victims of cultural fatigue. By telling themselves

---

[1]F. Stephen R. Donaldson. Lord Foul's Bane. (Ballantine Books: New York. 1977) p.199.

they will like everything, accept everyone and enjoy it all, they have successfully steeled themselves to survive a cross-cultural encounter without being hurt, and they now have little sympathy with the cross-cultural lifer suffering from cultural fatigue.

One of the more incredible responses to this phenomenon was chronicled in a denominational publication a few years ago. A summer youth missionary observed a stressed-out career missionary mother struggling with a silly little frustration in her world. Some thieves had broken in and taken a few household appliances. Wanting to place the incident in kingdom perspective, the summer missionary boasted, in print, of having set the poor thing straight. "I was able to encourage her by helping her to ask herself what difference this robbery will make ten years from now."

The perspective was right on. The timing was abysmal. People who have been in the trenches long enough to unpack their suitcases have had their bubble of isolation to another culture punctured long ago. They are no longer impervious to the hurt of being looked at, laughed at, borrowed from or lied to one time too often. They may have opened themselves up to the excruciating process of being rebuilt, but their cultural tolerance may have peaked or plateaued. Being lied to may be cute at first. ("They want to please so much they don't dare admit they don't know how to point you back to the hotel!") After you have been given misleading directions for three hours the novelty wears thin. Being lied to too many times can turn you sour on a culture.

One of the more discouraging discoveries I made as a first-term missionary was the number of third and fourth termers who seemed to have soured on the culture. There were those who seemed to have cultivated a pervasive cynicism about their hosts. Chronic complainers make lousy company but misery does love company. As I looked to my colleagues for encouragement with my own struggles in engaging the culture, I had hoped to see examples of well adjusted veterans who, with the years, had found that the differences between cultures were getting smaller. Gratefully, I met some who had been rebuilt. I also met some who had reached their tolerance threshold. My advice to eager short-termers or fresh first-termers is to keep your comments to yourself as you observe the strains of cultural fatigue in the lifers. They may not be in the mood for being rebuilt at the moment. Missions is a contact sport. Be sure of this: if you have no bruises you haven't been in the game long enough.

AN ORIENTATION EXERCISE

As I analyzed some of the frustrations of cross-cultural living, I made a catalogue of sixteen little stresses that had accumulated in my calendar. None of them seemed like major differences. Yet together, on occasion, they were capable of producing a severe case of cultural fatigue. Here are some of my personal pet peeves.

1. People parking in my driveway.
2. The stove repairman never returns with the parts for which you gave him money and the cabinet builder uses your cash deposit to build someone else's cabinet.
3. Getting a dial tone is a minor miracle; getting a phone repaired is a direct act of God.
4. People cashing checks in long, slow supermarket lines (some frustrations cross all cultural lines).
5. Erratic store hours keep you guessing as to when the bank closes, the butcher shop opens, and the beauty parlor reopens after siesta.

The most incredible combination of these little nuisances together on the wrong day became my cultural calvary. Yours will be different. No dry-run orientation can prepare you for what may occur but an orientation period could be devoted to how we may handle unexpected cultural collisions.

- ❑ Park a car erratically behind your tour leader's car in the church parking lot and observe his reaction from the second-story safety of the pastor's study. Better yet, park a car behind the pastor's car and video the reaction.
- ❑ Have members of your team deliberately arrive late to an orientation session to observe the reaction of others. Then debrief the group on their responses.

"When two world
views collide there are
bound to be bruises."

Chapter 3

FIRST IMPRESSIONS, FIRST DEPRESSIONS

THERE IS NOTHING LIKE THE IMMEDIACY OF A DIARY to record the experience of a cross cultural encounter. It was through this thermometer that I was able to monitor my response to life in a foreign culture and to gauge my growth in cultural awareness. It was not long before the bubbly enthusiasm of first impressions was tempered by the distinct hint of first depressions.

As a rookie missionary I traced my moods and impressions in a diary. Later I gathered some of those thoughts into a small pamphlet entitled: "(Almost) Everything you wanted to know about Missionaries but were afraid it might be true." Those first impressions, for the rawness and irreverence with which they were written, have a certain scientific value fifteen years later as they chronicle my pilgrimage through the murky waters of that first term.

As a short-term missionary or member of a visiting work group you may not experience all of these frustration factors, but this sampling of our "typical" days and most transparent moods may help you to identify with, minister to, and especially, pray for, a career missionary going through a

depression tunnel or showing signs of cultural withdrawal. And it may just surprise you how many of these lessons I learned fifteen years ago will still apply to your short-term or first-time experience in another culture.
And at least it will help you to ask the right questions.

People love to ask a missionary questions. Trouble is, it's not always that easy to come up with just the right questions. So don't get caught asking those worn-out favorites:

- "What do the people eat?"
- "Is it hot where you are?"
- "How does it feel to be back home?"

Why not engage in some truly heady inquiry by trying these questions on your missionary host.

1. WHAT IS THE MOST IMPORTANT THING YOU CAN BRING TO THE MISSION FIELD?

A sense of humor: the ability to laugh at yourself, and to laugh with your colleagues.

2. WHAT IS THE SECOND MOST IMPORTANT THING YOU CAN BRING TO THE MISSION FIELD?

A tender heart and the ability to empathize with others.

3. WHAT IS THE MOST DANGEROUS COMBINATION OF ATTITUDES YOU CAN DEVELOP ON THE MISSION FIELD?

The tendency to cry about the way the mission does things, and the tendency to laugh at the way the nationals do things.

4. WHEN DID YOU FIRST FEEL LIKE A REAL MISSIONARY?

I first had the feeling of being a real missionary as I was driving through the most incredible combination of pot-holes, ruts and creek beds imaginable. The dark clouds gathered and the rain spattered on the windshield of the little truck and I knew that we would be trapped back in the village for days if the road got any slipperier, and the creek bed rose any higher . . . and yet with the deep satisfaction that we had completed our mission.

It was then that I first realized we were actually in Ecuador, and the thought came to my mind that this must be what being a missionary was really like . . . that is until I remembered that our mission that afternoon had been to find a Christmas turkey, and it had taken longer than expected to catch and kill the thing.

5. WHEN DID YOU LEAST FEEL LIKE YOU WERE A MISSIONARY?

It happens off and on . . . mostly often! About halfway through reading my annual work goals the feeling will hit, or while filling out the car report. I have also had it happen while lying by a hotel pool under a hot sun, and it has even hit while lying in a pool of oil under a hot motor. There just doesn't seem to be any way to predict when the feeling may strike.

6. DO YOU HAVE TO FEEL LIKE A MISSIONARY TO BE ONE?

No, but you have to be a missionary to feel like one. By that I mean, don't think going to all the trouble of selling your video recorder, shooting yourself for a variety of mostly extinct tropical diseases, or landing at an airport where they ride shotgun on the fuel truck with machine guns will give you the feeling.

You can more likely get the missionary-feeling by inviting your neighbor to a Bible study, by enrolling in a practical evangelism program, or by praying with your pastor about a problem in the church.

7. WHAT IS THE BIGGEST MISTAKE YOU EVER MADE AS A MISSIONARY?

I would say it happened long before I ever got to the field . . . early in my college days. Since boyhood and into my teens I had been very regular in keeping a devotional time. My brother and I always kneeled by the bed at night to pray. But in college I chose the top bunk.

Anyone knows that is a fairly good excuse for not kneeling by your bed to pray. . . so I would just lay my head on my pillow and pray . . . and then as days went by, and studies got heavier, and hockey practices harder, I would just lay my head on the pillow and. . .

Once I had broken the rhythm of regular devotions, it was easier and easier "not to have them tonight," and I have been struggling to get back on my knees ever since. Neglecting personal devotions is always our biggest mistake.

8. WHAT ARE SOME OF THE MOST UNFORGETTABLE MOMENTS OF YOUR FIRST-TERM AS A MISSIONARY?

1) Most frightening moment . . .
2) Most embarrassing moment . . .
3) Most ego-building experience . . .

4) Biggest thrill . . .
5) Biggest let-down . . .
6) Biggest surprise . . .

9. WHAT WOULD YOU DESCRIBE AS YOUR MOST DIFFICULT CULTURAL ADJUSTMENT?

My first impression of Latin culture was of a society stifled by interminable paperwork. Everywhere I turned there seemed to be copies upon copies, signatures upon seals, stamps upon more stamps. The triplicate form was an obsolete necessity for almost every step of existence. There was no apparent logic to the madness . . . only the unerring belief that if one copy was good, ten would surely be better. For everything there was a stamp, and a signature (or two) for every purpose under heaven.

An army of two-fingered typists lead this daily onslaught against the inroads of efficiency. Wherever I needed a license, a birth certificate, or a customs release there was sure to be a line of people backed up behind these bureaucratic bottlenecks. The lines often spilled out of the building, and into the street.

The Spanish word for "paperwork" or "red tape" is *"tramite."* Pronounced, it has the uncanny ring of the English word "trauma." The end result was often not unsimilar. For example, it took seven cross town trips to the traffic department, and 8-10 hours standing in line to renew my driver's license. That is something that a career missionary will face more often than a short term worker, but the trauma of "tramite" is an inevitable part of learning to survive in a developing nation. How we react to "the way they do things" will be even harder to swallow when one is on a "short term" leash. After all, I only have 35 more days to get the job done and here they are holding me up by this insane red tape.

10. WHAT IS AN AVERAGE DAY LIKE IN THE LIFE OF A MISSIONARY?

There is no typical day in the life of a cross cultural explorer. It might be helpful to realize that even on a short term assignment you will not be immune from having a bad day. You may find comfort in classifying each day's experience into one of three general classes of days, as I did.

CLASS 1 DAYS: Those days when you feel like "Wonder "Missionary"

CLASS 2 DAYS: Those days when you wonder if this is what it really means to be a missionary.

CLASS 3 DAYS: Days when you feel it's a wonder they ever let you be a missionary.

In order for you to get the idea here's how a few of my first term days were spent.

TYPICAL CLASS 1 DAYS:

Days when you feel like "Wonder Missionary"

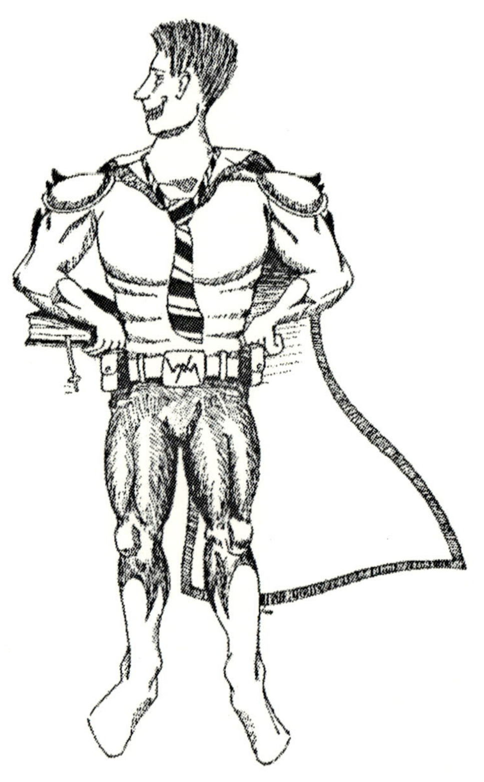

April 29/81

Study in preparation for making up SEAN tests. Servio, our provincial worker, and clan arrived with Narcissa. Hope made dinner for everybody. Servio and I visited two new Christians who had accepted the Lord yesterday in LaToma. Hope went to ladies meeting with Narcissa and Carmen while Servio and I babysat. Manuel arrived at 6:30 for a nice visit and we talked about his pastor Cesar's narrow approach. Tried to encourage him to consider leading a group in Catacocha. Then Nancy and Victor arrived for marriage counseling and I dealt with them until 9 pm while Hope fed and entertained Manuel. Like she said today: "Today I feel like a real missionary."

CLASS II DAYS:

Wondering if this is what it really means to be a missionary

November 30/81

Terrible day of nagging problems. Plane late and didn't get back from La Toma till noon. My request for a ham license at the Radio Club has been denied. Fixing a leaking faucet until 8 at night.

January 13/81

Today was my baptism in how to get a parcel out of customs.

1.Take parcel notice to back of post office for instructions.
2.Go to outside stamp vendor for stamps.
3.Back to post office for more instructions.
4.To collection office for customs forms.
5.Back to the post office for more instructions.
6.To customs office for signatures.(8 blocks)
7.To the Central Bank for 8 sucre payment.(7 blocks)
8.Back to the customs for official stamp(7 blocks)
9.Back to the post office for ... the PACKAGE!

Two hours, 4 offices, and 31 blocks later I have six parcels from home. . . worth it but what an ordeal! Received telegram of the poisoning death of 4 Poma children. . . a Christian family in Orianga.

May 25/81

To TAME airline office for tickets, only to find out that there probably won't be a plane tomorrow.
To POST OFFICE with 15 letters to discover that they won't be selling stamps today.
To MARKET for peanuts to find out they are sold out.
To MIRROR SHOP . . . closed!
To pay HYDRO ELECTRIC BILL . . . success at last!
To MECHANIC for 6th time to see about fog light protector. . . not in for the 5th time.

October 14/80

A sad time getting the kids on the plane. . . the parting was not difficult, praise the Lord, but the empty house was terrible. . . putting away toys, bikes, clothes, beds they have used, hanging up the welcome sign till next time. Joel was sad all day talking about Peter and Jennifer and going to get them again. Our first staff prayer meeting with the Johnsons helped.

October 13/82

Provincial worker in town . . . sharing the uprising of false accusations against him . . . stayed for dinner. Joel started school today. Spent the afternoon doing car reports and babysitting while Hope went to ladies meeting.

Joel was my only helper as I showed "Pilgrim's Progress" to 500 cavalry recruits. Hope is discouraged about her lost purse and the state of the church here. The feeling is mutual.

CLASS III DAYS

The ones you've all been waiting for, those days when you feel that it's a wonder they ever let you be a missionary (and maybe wish you weren't)

April 13/81

Rotten day . . . wife uncooperative, no sports report on radio, no spiritual food, and no drive. After the service a meeting of Sunday School teachers kept me longer than I wanted and Hope was asleep when I got home. Amazing how rotten life is when we don't get what we want. Good lesson on the "old man" today.

October 8/81

Had a crabby day...

- physically tired
- emotionally exhausted
- financial pinch
- crowded desk

And the bank can't tell you what you have in your account until tomorrow.

November 22/82

A rather "down" day when you start to wonder what you are doing here.

11. WHAT ARE YOU REALLY DOING THERE?

We are trying to keep Class III days to a minimum and make all the little opportunities that each Class II day presents count for eternity. Class I days are pure cream.

12. DO MISSIONARIES EVER HAVE ANY FUN?

Two day back-packing treks are now available providing breath-taking views complete with a variety of daring river crossings and mule accompaniment. . . but you may be required to carry tracts or Bibles along, which automatically qualifies as "mission mileage" on your quarterly itinerating report, and so should not be technically considered "FUN" since it more properly fits in the category of "WORK" right in there with overdue mission reports.

You may also be asked to play basketball on a local team, take part in a street soccer match with the neighbors, speak at a young peoples' picnic, or be obliged to sit through televised World Cup matches with Alliance Youth Corps guests (or other less committed types of visitors). All such activities including teaching UNO to the local pastor, learning guitar chords from the lady next door, or playing table tennis with her daughter, by the sheer linguistic and cultural nature of the event, are really only borderline "FUN" and more correctly qualify as "definite missionary WORK." (see missionary handbook page 50)

FOOTNOTE to future generations of FIRST TERMERS: It is to the missionary's advantage to have as much FUN as possible, since whatever qualifies as WORK must be duly reported to superiors. They are not interested in how much FUN is being done.

13. DO MISSIONARIES EVER DO ANY WORK?

In my case an annual narrative report is due December 15, and regular progress reports are required to evaluate your yearly work plan (due August 31). A mileage and vehicle report is expected every 3 months. Language reports, film reports, work special reports, and conference reports cannot be overlooked. Reporting on the "WORK" is a very important aspect of "THE WORK."

14. WHAT IS THE TOUGHEST THING ABOUT BEING A MISSIONARY?

Living up to the expectations and output of other colleagues, and then living with yourself when you didn't.

15. WHAT DID YOU LEARN DURING YOUR FIRST TERM?

- a smattering of survival Spanish
- some sneaky shortcuts to filling out car reports
- a few creative ways to get a truck unstuck from the mud
- that it will take a whole lot longer than one term to get this job done.

16. HAVE YOU EVER FELT LIKE YOU'D LIKE TO PACK UP AND HEAD HOME?

YES

17. DID YOU EVER WISH YOU HADN'T COME?

NO

18. HOW DID YOU EVER GET TO BE A MISSIONARY?

I have had occasion to wonder that myself. Most of us have a sneaking suspicion that we somehow slipped through the cracks of the screening process. Now that we are here we realize that the cracks were wider than we imagined.

The early disappointment with colleagues (their commitment to the cause, their acceptance of the culture, their dedication to the Lord, their conduct on the Conference floor) leads us to suspect that others do not exactly fit the sacred stereotype either. That is when first impressions may drift into first depressions. From the lofty perspective of a fourth term veteran I share my first impressions of life in another culture with any who might be tempted to ask, “Is there life after the first-term experience?” The fact that I have stayed on is part of my personal quest to satisfactorily answer that question.

The jolts you receive as you begin to suspect that the hallowed missionary is just an empty myth will probably be part of your first cross-cultural encounter. You will almost always be more disappointed with your colleagues and missionary hosts than you are with the people they have come to reach. Getting over that hurdle is a necessary step toward effective cross cultural ministry. Staying long enough to let those glorious first impressions be counterpoised by the inevitable first depressions is an essential rung on the ladder to satisfactory short-term service.

PRACTICAL POINTERS for short-termers who suspect that their missionary hosts are having more than their share of Class III days.

- Don’t pry! Don’t look for what isn’t there. Most missionaries live in victory and handle stress very well.
- Don’t preach! Your silent example of patience in a problem situation will do much more to encourage, or rebuke, your host sponsor, than any sermon on self-control.

AN ORIENTATION EXERCISE

Keep a faithful diary of your feelings and responses in everyday situations before you begin your cross-cultural encounter. Writing down how you react under pressure, and how you want to react, will reduce the drag of depression, when you disappoint yourself in a strange cultural setting where you had hoped to handle things better.

Place in descending order the following factors that tend to most upset you, and discuss with your mission orientation group how to be ready to respond to each. Which of these situations will most likely turn your glorious first impressions into a fit of major depression?

_____ a flat tire when we are late for a ministry engagement.

_____ an evasive answer by our host missionary to a genuine question from our group.

_____ a missionary who puts creature comfort ahead of a clear ministry opportunity.

_____ a paperwork or red tape delay that alters our work schedule.

_____ a lazy host who resigns himself to not seeking a creative solution to a problem in our group by blaming the culture.

_____ missing a chance to go with the group on an extra in-depth cultural experience because of personal tiredness or sickness.

_____ having our project fall short of completion because of a group member's illness.

"You may be more disappointed with your colleagues and missionary hosts than with the people they have come to serve."

Chapter 4

THE COST FACTOR

MISSIONS IS A WORTHY CAUSE because we serve a worthy Christ. World evangelization is an extravagant operation. But what about the waste factor? People who are thinking of participating in short-term missions experience often face the issue in a very direct way.

How can I justify this major expenditure when there is a shortfall in our denominational missions coffers? A single air fare to most countries could put five national pastors through seminary, or build country churches for an entire congregation or two. Is the cost of traveling to see the mission field for two or three weeks really a wise investment? These are hard questions.

As a career missionary who sees the enormous needs on the field, I can still say that the investment in short-term missions is definitely worth it. For some biblical undergirding of my argument, consider Matthew 26:6-14 where a woman pours expensive perfume on Jesus' head. The disciples question such a lavish expression of love. "What's the point of the waste?" they grumble. Jesus answers their protest by infusing a very intimate moment in his personal ministry with an unexpected missionary twist. The essence of his reasoning is that the perceived "waste" was worth it, because the object of her affection was worthy.

There have been times when I have asked the disciples' question. . . when I have wondered personally about the "waste."

- Is it really worth it to slog through muddy roads, take bone-wrenching mule rides, hike hot hills, or sleep on board beds?
- Is it worth it to trek and teach, or to say goodbye to your children for weeks at a stretch?

Remember the three diary classifications of my days:

Class 1: Days when you feel like Wonder Missionary

Class 2: Days when you wonder if this is really what it means to be a missionary

Class 3: Days when you wonder how they ever let you be a missionary in the first place.

When I would come to the end of a day, and conclude that this was another one of those Class 3 days, I would ask questions about the "waste".

- Are the people who sacrifice to send me here, and to keep me on the field, really getting their money's worth?
- What about our parents who have given up their grandchildren so we could be here?
- What about those faithful givers?

The only sane conclusion I can come to at those times is that, in any enterprise, the "waste" is only worth it if the goal is great enough. Million dollar television cameras and sophisticated moon buggies were left littering the face of the moon, because the goal of placing men on the moon was deemed great enough to warrant the sacrifice.

Jesus' response to the disciples' question was similar. The waste, as they called it, was worth it because the goal was great enough. The object of the woman's extravagant expression of affection was worthy of the cost she expended. Watchman Nee wrote, "The idea of WASTE only comes into our Christianity when we underestimate the WORTH of our Lord." The disciples' point about the poor was valid. Jesus did not dismiss the poor. They would always be there, and their needs ought to be addressed. But the Master redirected their focus to the overriding issue of His presence. "You will not always have me."

The Problem of the Poor: A Case for Common Sense

If you weigh the cost of a short-term missions venture against the needs of the poor you encounter along the way, the guilt will overcome you. You will never come. So how do we answer the argument, "This could have been given to the poor"? Let me try.

There are voices in North American circles who attempt to address the issue from behind library stacks and college lecterns. One recognized missions expert tried to make a point for the poor by analyzing the standard for square feet of living quarters allowed Southern Baptist missionaries. I see no correlation between ministry effectiveness and broadloom carpet. The insidious tug of materialism is a constant in every Christian's life, missionaries included.

One woman who has walked across our living room carpet in Ecuador is Carmen, a poor pastor's wife. Her kitchen is a collage of odd Tupperware and teacups passed on from my wife and other colleagues. Beyond occasional small gifts, we help her very little. But the hours spent in our living room pouring out her problems have produced in Carmen an unusual reaction. She no longer sees the carpet, the VCR, the cable TV, or the computer, that clutter our lives. She comes to visit my wife, not for handouts or loans, but "because you are my only friend," she says through tears.

Compassion is a matter of the heart. There are mission service agencies who come to this country to dispense compassion like eye drops. The Guayaquil "suburbs," as they are known, are vast, flat tracts of land-filled swamp where squatters' shacks have been gradually incorporated into the city grid. In these down and out areas, local churches have welcomed aid from outside. Some foreign funds are channeled to individual congregations to provide breakfast programs and school supplies to children of the neighborhood. A school may operate in the church. The only requirement is attendance at the church Sunday School.

So what effect does this social aid have on the advance of the Gospel? The first people to see through this facade of cosmetic compassion are the local believers themselves. The story you hear from them is a recurring theme. The bulk of the money is turned over to church leaders to administer the program. When there is the possibility of augmenting a miserly salary, what layman would not be interested? Yet the result is a drain on lay leadership at the local church level. Almost any lay person will prefer to be involved in administering a school program for remuneration, rather than an evangelism program for the sheer love of the Lord.

A second spin-off of these aid programs is that the children who attend begin to confuse Christianity with having to come to Sunday School. When and if they make a decision to follow Christ, their understanding of discipleship becomes reduced to following a list of rules and regulations. As adults, it is hard to divorce genuine Christian commitment from the legalistic brand learned as a child.

A third pitfall of such programs is that international quotas can be placed on local pastors to produce more "poor people". Pastors feel pressure to add people to their rolls in order to keep receiving the aid from outside, so that the church rosters become cluttered with semi-Christians, who are in it for the take. In the end, in many cases, the charity institution that funnels money into the local church begins to determine the church's agenda. It is harder to hear the voice of the Spirit telling the Body to add a night for evangelism training when the people who write the checks are requesting a night for parent-teacher association meetings.

So before you opt for cashing in your ticket to Africa to support a needy child or open a school breakfast program, consider this. The "cup of water" Jesus used as a symbol of basic human compassion is a very spontaneous personal expression. So often, we want to do it all by long distance. (*Our lines are open today. Call this toll free number and you can do something today for this poor child's tomorrow.*) The truth of the matter is that a good percentage of this long-reach aid gets lost in the reaching.

Let me belabor the point a little longer. Jesus told John's disciples to "report to John what you have seen and heard".

> *"The blind receive sight, the lame walk, those who have leprosy are cured, the deaf hear, the dead are raised, and the good news is preached to the poor."*
>
> Luke 7:22

The lucky poor! The blind get to see, the lame get to walk, the lepers get healed, the deaf get to hear, the dead get new life, and the poor. . . well, the poor get Bibles. If you follow the logic of the lesson, everyone else gets their physical needs met, so you would expect Jesus to end by saying that the poor get free breakfasts, or the poor get school textbooks, or the poor get rich. Instead, he says that the poor get the Gospel preached to them. I don't think the Lord could be much clearer.

The shortest, toughest route to true Christianity is to preach Christ, to pray for healing and to teach faith. I listened to my seminary "Theology of the Church" students, who were pastors and lay leaders, reject categorically the idea of massive aid from the exterior as a solution to the social needs of their people. To a man, they reaffirmed the role of the local church in fulfilling the social needs peculiar to their own people. Their plea was for a personal relationship with the poor. We cannot bypass the personal reach of a cup of water. A cup of water is passed from one hand to another. The impact of that image should never be lost. Water is still a fairly inexpensive commodity. The secret is not WHAT is given, as much as the WAY it is given.

The "rationing" approach to aid is always inadequate. We will never have enough to give everyone just a little. All we manage to do is dilute the Gospel we have come to share. The "personal touch" approach is the only satisfactory way to administer a cup of water. One brimming cup at a time, to one needy life at a time, seems to be the system our Savior endorsed. There is no real sense in trying to reach across a continent to help a hungry child, if I am not willing to reach across a room to hand a cup of water to a neighbor in need.

> *I was in bed with the flu and you brought a box of cookies over.*
> *I was out of work and could not pay the water bill, so you called and had it reconnected.*
> *I had eight kids at home on a welfare check, so you let me go through the used clothing closet at your church.*
> *I was not feeling well enough to care for myself, and you put my name on the list for Meals on Wheels.*
> *I was in jail for child abuse and you came with the chaplain to give me help.*

Having just been showered with a luxurious gift, the Lord Jesus Christ, who loves and knows the needs of the poor better than any, receives the gift with grace. Far from rebuking the extravagance, he corrects the misconception that every penny we have should be showered on the poor. He does not agree with their assessment of the situation as a "waste." Instead he praises it as an "investment" in His Kingdom.

There are times

There are times when I have wondered about the "waste." Sometimes it's "wasted" time. After planning a major trek to the interior for months, a foul-up in communication left me standing at a bus depot with two tickets and no travel partner. The delay in going to get him in another city set us back a whole day.

Once I left a driver's license at a police control checkpoint. To replace it cost eight hours of paperwork and standing in lines over the course of a full week. Another time, all the family passports and a camera were taken from our vehicle while traveling to visit our children. Instead of getting away at 5:00 am in order to be with the kids that same day, we were forced to backtrack, replace documents and head out again at 4:00 in the afternoon for the all-night drive to Quito.

Sometimes it's wasted money. A missionary associate carpenter was flying from Quito to southern Ecuador to supervise a church construction project. The night before we were to go, I received word that the bulldozer had not done the necessary ground work. There was no sense in having the carpenter come. But he had already begun the first leg of his trip.

When I met him at the plane it was only to buy him a ticket back to Quito, using limited building funds for the purpose.

Or it can be wasted opportunities. After an all day drive to an isolated settlement we set up the generator and projector in time for an evening evangelistic program. The town poured out into the public square but when the projector was switched on, the bulb burned out. A replacement bulb also popped in seconds. There were no more, and the crowd whistled its protest as the equipment was packed for the return trip.

A king named Amaziah hired 100,000 Israeli mercenaries to help him consolidate his territory. He settled with the soldiers for 100 talents of silver. It was a hefty contract, but it was no sooner signed than a prophet piped up: "O King Amaziah, God told me to tell you not to take those Israelis along. You can if you want but you'll lose if you do."

Amaziah argued back: "But what will we do about the 100 talents I have just turned over to the troops?" I have asked the question myself, when I plan an Institute at which not a single person shows up, when I organize a film festival only to have local leadership scrap the idea, or when a national strike interrupts the youth retreat I had been working on for weeks. The prophet's answer to Amaziah's legitimate concern about the "waste" has given me perspective on these and other apparently bad investments. The prophet reminded the concerned king, worried about the loss of a minor fortune, "*The Lord has much more to give you than this.*" (2 Chronicles 25:9)

When you are tempted to wonder if the investment in a short-term missions adventure is worth the money that will be poured into tickets, hotels, meals and supplies (not to mention the time drain on the missionaries who receive you), it is good to remind yourself that the would-be "waste" is always worth it, if the goal is great enough. "*The Lord has much more to give you than this.*" And if you're concerned about lost business, lost clients, lost revenue, lost time or lost opportunities, keep squarely in view that "*The Lord has much more to give you than this.*"

Whatever may be your concern or situation, the issue of commitment to world missions, no matter how short, cannot be evaluated in what it will cost you, but in what it has already cost Him. The pouring out of an expensive perfume seemed to the disciples to be an outlandish extravagance. The Scripture says they were more than just a little upset by what they deemed indiscriminate waste. The Bible says they were actually "indignant." Their pragmatic solution sounded so sensible. . . sell the stuff and make use of good hard cash to help the poor. The trouble was they were looking at the wrong bottom line.

You may have no idea where the money will come from to finance your dream of hands-on action in a foreign mission field. The idea will never make sense in dollars and cents. The real bottom line of any investment in this very extravagant enterprise of world evangelization, no matter how limited, is not what it will cost you, but what it has already cost Him. The financial feasibility of the missionary enterprise can only be accurately measured in terms of the worth of the One we serve, not in terms of the apparent "wastes" involved.

A century ago, a young man was touring British churches with a burning burden for missions. He was looking for Christians who would support him financially in this high risk ideal of reaching another part of the world for Christ. At the close of a meeting a friend slipped out of the crowd, took his hand, and slipped in a five pound note. "Seeing it's for you, Robert," he said magnanimously, "Here's something for your support." In those days the gift was very generous but Robert returned the bill.

"If it's just for me Jack, I can't take it." The friend was taken aback, but recovering and realizing his mistake, he pulled a second five pound note from his pocket. "Well, seeing it's for Him, Robert, here's ten." "*It is the Lord Christ you serve.*"

There will always be someone ready to remind you of the "waste," but if you choose to do it for Him, He will not forget your faith investment. The exciting conclusion to the incident is contained in the stunning words of the Lord: "*Wherever this gospel is preached in the whole world, what she has done will be spoken in memory of her.*" The love gift to the Lord had universal repercussions: "WHEREVER this gospel is preached in the WHOLE WORLD." What this woman did in sacrifice to Christ was inscribed in the pages of Scripture for all posterity, so that in every culture and every country where God's Word is read, down through the centuries, Christ continues to keep his word to that woman. Her act of love is honored, and Jesus Christ is glorified all over again. You will find that the Lord has a way of taking the little we spend on Him, and using it to literally touch the ends of the earth.

You can be sure that what you invest in Christ's Kingdom, by way of time and money will never be lost. It will not be "wasted." The "waste" will always be worth it, because the goal of getting the Gospel to every creature is worthy of everything we have to give.

AN ORIENTATION EXERCISE

Below is a checklist of possible perfumes I could pour out to Christ to serve Him in short-term missions. Which of these would it most please the Lord for me to give up in order to invest in the worthy enterprise of world missions?

- ❑ a savings account earmarked for retirement.
- ❑ a recreation budget or club membership.
- ❑ an investment portfolio.
- ❑ an annual vacation I have earned.
- ❑ a leave of absence I have coming me.
- ❑ something I enjoy but don't really need.
- ❑ a job opportunity finally within any grasp.

Chapter 5

THE TREASURE CHEST

SEPARATIONS ARE ALWAYS PAINFUL, no matter how short. Family separations are a fact of the missionary experience. Even short-term personnel face the issue of saying good-bye. More able experts than I have documented the fact that family separation is a grief experience. One copes with a separation as he does with GRIEF. There is the denial, even anger, then guilt, and finally the acceptance. While you may only be contemplating a three-month medical mission to Malaysia, the separations involved with short-term mission experience may be profound. We have no guarantee that things will be the same when we get back.

The morning of the day we were moving out of our house for return to the field after our first furlough, we received a phone call that my wife's father had suffered a heart attack. One week before we were scheduled to leave for the field, he passed away. Despite a two-week extension we still left with my wife in a very tender stage of the grieving process. In the first year back on the field both my only brother and only sister were married. I was unable to share those happiest days of their lives with them.

Understandably, the majority of short-term missions candidates will not experience such traumatic separation issues. However, the principles of this chapter that are shared from the perspective of a career missionary may equally apply to a two-week internship in an Indian village of northern Canada. For some who venture to try their wings at cross-cultural ministry as a result of reading this book, the experience of separation may be even more excruciating. The career missionary has no monopoly on the pain of separations, short or long.

Mother's Day comes and goes. Father's Day, anniversaries, birthdays, Thanksgiving Day, Christmas and New Year's Eve, along with all the familiar traditions, are times when we cannot be together. Understanding what is going on emotionally during these extended separations helps us to deal with it as a normal, though painful, part of life. We can learn to deal with it though we may never enjoy it!

Every goodbye leaves a gouge in our world. There is a vacuum, a blank space where the other person used to be, a chair at the table, a slot in the toothbrush holder, an empty bedroom, a vacant window, a pillow on the floor, a bench on the dock where Grampa used to sit. As the person passes on, we reserve that space physically, and emotionally in our lives and in our schedules. But gradually, unconsciously, that space begins to close in on itself.

People who ask us, sympathetically, "How could you ever send your kids away to a boarding school?" are searching to understand an experience they may not have had. I have attempted to avoid the question by responding, "We don't send them away, we leave them at a school where they are cared for deeply and ministered to richly." But that doesn't help my personal hurt. How have we learned to handle it?

When the kids flew back to boarding school we would leave the house strewn with toys for a while, leave their beds unmade and their chairs at the table. The first day after a long weekend or a holiday visit was a real downer. Yet many missionaries who have had to leave their children in a boarding situation have secretly confessed to us what we also have felt. There were actually entire days that went by when I barely thought of my children. Was I an unusual father, a delinquent Dad, because my heart wasn't bleeding constantly for my kids? No! The separation-grief experience was merely taking its natural course. We are neither physically nor psychologically constructed to live with an open grief wound forever. God has made us with merciful mechanisms for getting over good-byes.

I write these words from my experience of separation in the hopes of encouraging some wavering soul who is dying to step out into a short-term cross cultural adventure but doesn't think he or she can stand the pain of leaving the boyfriend, or the kids, or the dog, for ten days in Timbuktu, or three years in Russia.

The Trust Test

God's solutions for the hurt of human separation and loss are not simply psychological. The greatest resource for handling human pain is

God himself. The lessons I am learning about trusting God have been woven into the fabric of my life from an early age. I am gradually becoming comfortable with the fact that you can trust God with your most precious treasures. For any candidate to cross-cultural ministry, the separations involved require us to grow in our trust of God.

Let me suggest four trust tests that God uses to help us trust Him in ever widening circles of our existence. The Lord begins His trust test with the little things, then takes us on to trusting Him in larger things. From there the Lord asks us to trust Him with the loves of our life. Finally, He wants to move us into the mode of total trust, where we will trust Him with our very life itself. I'd like to illustrate these lessons from my personal pilgrimage because the experience of crossing cultures is very often one of the gates to learning to trust God more.

The Little Things

I'm glad I learned to trust God with the little things. When I was eight years old I lived on a large western Canadian farm. It was a lot of real estate on which to lose a wallet. I lost my wallet with my total lifetime portfolio: $1.85.

I made the loss a matter of personal challenge to God. If He was God He would help me find that wallet and its contents. A year and one long winter passed. I prayed and trusted with what some would call "childlike faith." Whatever kind it was, it was real. It would have taken a massive dose of most adult faith to believe that the wallet and its contents would ever be seen again.

The large melt-off of an exceptionally heavy winter produced a minor lake in the pasture in front of the farm yard. Spring came and the water receded to a small reservoir. One day, trudging through the pasture after having gone to "get the cows", I was scuffing through the dried bed left by the spring run-off, kicking at the clods of mud made by the feet of the cattle. Then it happened! Miracle of miracles, my toe came through one more clod and unearthed an object, mud-caked but clearly recognizable. I stooped and picked up a perfectly intact leather wallet and opened it to confirm that it still contained one dollar and eighty five cents. As if I ever doubted.

The lesson was clear. My treasures, all $1.85 worth, were safe with Him. It was an early indicator that God could be trusted with my treasures. He was telling me gently that he could be trusted with little things and that there was nothing too small for Him to manage.

Larger Things

It was later that I learned to trust God with larger things. When my high school gang headed off for universities across the country I set out for Bible College with an undefined orientation toward a Christian ministry career. In taking that step I was sure I was giving up a university education, a respectable profession, a real job.

In my first year at Bible College the institution took a bold step to work toward seminary status. They needed a group of guinea pigs who would step onto a university campus, through which they were making the application, and pursue an undergraduate degree. I was one of the initial group of twenty who made the move.

Marriage and a delay in seminary accreditation allowed me not only to complete my bachelor's degree but also to finish a Master's degree as well, and work for a year as a high school English teacher. I began to observe that I could never really give up anything for God but that He had a way of giving back everything I ever gave Him.

A missionary statesman of the past was once asked why he was giving up a promising position. "Is it the salary? Is the salary not big enough?" the company executive asked.

"No, the salary is plenty big, bigger than I could have ever dreamed of," he replied.

"Then what is it? Why can't you accept our offer?"

His answer was simple. "It's the job." He said. "The job's just not big enough."

Today as a career missionary I am certain there are those who wonder why I never got a real job. But as I look at the options that were open to me along the way, to accept the fellowship for Ph.D. studies, to head the English department of a High School, or to accept an assistant professorship and a Director of Athletics offer from the college president, I had little trouble narrowing my focus to what had become by then a solid conviction. I wanted to be a missionary. It is the only job that would be big enough to satisfy my total needs as a person and to keep me challenged for a lifetime. It was the only real job that was big enough for me.

Take a look at my job for size. The perks are incredible. International travel, a fresh start every four years, constant mobility, all moving expenses paid, a company car, private schooling for my kids at a premium institution (the envy of the international set in a city of a million and a half), a college allowance for my kids and a Christmas trip home their first year in college to anywhere in the world their parents happen to be. Then a month vacation with pay and my company pays the travel, a sabbatical every four years, and a job in which I can virtually write my own job description. I hate to exaggerate what I enjoy and I don't want to paint a picture of opulent extravagance among missionaries, but personally my mission takes good care of me, and when I get down on my world it helps to put this positive turn on my lifestyle so that I begin to see, again, the tremendous advantage of living under the watchful eye of a generous God.

I, for one, should be able to say with confidence that you can trust God with the larger things of your life. We are somehow afraid that if we give in to God he will always take the bigger slice! There may be people who have never plugged into the privilege of shorter term missions assignments, or even considered a more drastic career shift, for fear of what they might lose in terms of retirement benefits or job security. Let me encourage you that God can be trusted with the larger things of your life.

The Loves of my Life

I have also been learning that I can trust God with the loves of my life. I love to write. Little did I imagine that the deep-rooted craving to express myself in print would be completely satisfied as a missionary. I have opportunities to prepare sermons, contribute articles, produce educational materials, and even to express myself acceptably in a second language. A language-learning translation project in my first term became the grist for a history book, *Daybreak Over Ecuador.* A series of sermons and talks that were given during furlough ministries, and supervision of short-term work teams are the raw material for this book. A centennial celebration of the denomination in Ecuador was the occasion for editing the first Spanish history of our national church.

But I have other loves. I recall the day during our second term when my wife, Hope, was to go in for testing for a potential tumor while I was going out the door on a four-day trip into the back country. The children were miles away in dorm school. *My wife needs me*, I rationalized, *and here I am going off to teach a Bible Institute in the jungle.* Can I trust Him to take care of my treasures?

As I sat feeling sorry for myself in the dim lamp light of the evening evangelistic service in the jungle province of Zamora-Chinchipe, totally disconnected from phone and family, and wondering what the results of my wife's tests would be, the Lord spoke, directly and personally, through the public reading of Scripture.

> *"No plague, pestilence, disaster will come near your dwelling."*
> Psalm 91: 3-6; 9-11

Perhaps the congregation had not read loud enough, or well enough, or perhaps, just perhaps, I had not heard it clearly enough. In any event, the service leader asked the group to stand and repeat the entire Scripture reading. There are times when this kind of overkill would have annoyed me. Not tonight. With strong reassurance the Lord was repeating his promise, just for me.

> *"No plague, pestilence, or disaster will come near your dwelling."*

I was safe in His care. He could be trusted with the loves of my life. I returned home later to the happy news that the growths were benign; and the comforting realization that the Lord had known it all along.

I have other loves. Being assigned to Ecuador left open the ever so tempting possibility that mission leaders would assign us to the city of Quito. Quito is the home of the Alliance Academy, where missionaries from many missions in several Latin American countries send their children to receive a quality North American education. An allocation to Quito would mean we could have our cake and eat it too. We could serve the Lord as full-time missionaries while our children lived right at home with us.

It was January in Costa Rica. We had reached the watershed of the language school experience when the fateful letter arrived from our field executive committee. "You have been tentatively appointed to Loja."

Loja is Ecuador's southern most city. You cannot get further away from the capital of Quito and still be in Ecuador! Again the issue was clear: Can I trust Him with my treasures? With the loves of my life?

The letter would have been a difficult pill to swallow had it not been for a word from the Lord that very morning in my regular devotions. God's timing is impeccable. The verse that stood out to me that morning as I read was Mark 10:29:

> *"I tell you the truth, Jesus replied, no one who has left home or brothers or sisters or mother or father or children or fields for me and the gospel will fail to receive a hundred times as much in this present age (homes, brothers, sisters, mothers, children, and fields and with them, persecutions) and in the age to come, eternal life."*

The promise that I grasped for at the time was the last part. "In the age to come, eternal life." "Lord," I bargained, "If you really mean what you say, (that if I or my family make these kinds of sacrifices you will guarantee me that they will be your children and receive eternal life"), I suppose we will learn to live with the temporary separations. The assignment to Loja was accepted in the clear confirmation of God's promise. It was only later that I came to realize the promise had much broader ramifications.

Other Mothers

Jennifer had not reached her sixth birthday when we left her in the Alliance dorm and went on to Loja to begin our ministry. Two months later she and her brother made their first visit to our new home for a long weekend. "Mommy, now I have three mothers" she reported triumphantly at the table. Two other dorm moms had come into her life to minister to her in motherly ways. It was the first clue of more such moms to come. Since Pat and Lucy have come Ruth and Wanneta, Maxine and Marj, and Pam, and countless other women who have moved into Jennifer's life for shorter or longer periods to be a mom when Mom could not be there. . . not replacement mothers, but extensions of Mom.

Through the years other mothers have been there. Besides the dorm moms are the adopted moms. Women from our supporting churches of Canada have adopted our family, pray for them regularly, send cards on birthdays and occasional packages. There is no way of knowing who they all are, but often a letter reminds us that, somewhere out there, many women are having a motherly prayer ministry to my daughter. While I will never know them all, I choose to believe that the Lord has arranged at least a hundred mothers for my children. After all, that is what the promise says: "*No one will leave father or mother. . . but will receive a hundred times. . . mothers. . .*"

The text also says that leaving brothers and sisters for the Lord's sake and the Gospel will qualify you to receive a hundred more from the Lord. It did not take us long to realize that the deep and lasting relationships built around the dorm life bond were producing brothers and sisters for life. Today as our children travel around the country, phone calls from Washington or Indiana or Texas are reminders that they have a royal heritage. Their extended family is flung about the globe, but there is always someone asking about someone else, a sure sign that sibling ties are strong and lasting.

The very literal fulfillment of this incredible promise in Mark was never made more clear to me than when I began to move about North America on church tour ministries. One of the negatives of missionary life is not having a house to call home. This lack of a permanent place can be unsettling to some, but we live with the advantages: no taxes, no mortgages, no roof repairs, no neighborhood problems. We are free to move at a moment's notice. The nomadic nature of the missionary does not appeal to everyone; even for one who confesses to enjoying the gypsy lifestyle the yearning for a yard of my own comes calling time and again. After all, one's home is one's castle and there is a little king in all of us.

However, the promise was also made that whoever leaves "home" for my sake and the Gospel's will receive a hundred *homes* as well. A hundred homes! But how?

Our Costa Rica language school apartment had a private yard with swing and banana trees. Our apartment home in Loja had a fireplace, roof deck, family room, rich wood-inlaid tile floors, and tons of kitchen cupboards. The living room window looked out on a green mountain side splashed with cactus and eucalyptus.

Our first apartment home in Guayaquil had no less than six color-coordinated bathrooms complete with bidets (which we discovered made fine flower planters, or foot washers for the kids). When the landlord terminated the contract, the Lord had arranged for a retired missionary resident in the city to relocate so that we could move into her colonial style mansion complete with massive towering palm trees and thirteen foot ceilings. I remember visiting the house at one time and drooling over the cool feel of the dark green stone-tile floors and the hammock swinging on the white tile veranda dressed with ample tropical greenery. It always seemed so cool, so fresh, so inviting, in the hot humid coastal climate. And now this historical home, selectively protected by the cultural patrimony of the nation, was our home. Television crews dropped by to ask if they could do filming in the home. . . at least until they saw our hand-built provincial missionary decor inside. And they came even less when we put up a tree house in the enormous rubber tree on the front lawn.

If the Lord has anything, he has a sense of humor. "I said a hundred homes and I mean to keep my word, whether you want them or not." If our residences on the field have not been enough proof, our furlough homes have further convinced us that the Lord is looking out for us. Just months before our first furlough He called a telephone repair man and his family to accept a short-term missions assignment to Central America so his house would be vacant for us. It was in the exact city for the exact period of time that we would need to be there. The house came complete with dishwasher, linens and a dog named Towser, a mammoth mutt who laid his chin DOWN on the table while we ate. As you contemplate the risks of accepting God's call to a short-term missions assignment, do not underestimate the rewards He may have in mind, for you and others.

To provide a furlough home for our family the second term it was necessary for the Lord to get a retired Christian and his wife to take a year in their motor home, traveling around the country, so that we could stay in their home. The Lord's assignments are tough, aren't they? This time the house came complete with dishwasher but, gratefully, no dog.

Some of God's choice people are not those who gave up having things to serve Him somewhere else, but people who, having things, gave them up to His servants. This second furlough home had a fine backyard where we felt free to flood our own family ice rink, and in so doing set back the grass an entire season.

If the field residences and furlough homes were not enough to convince me that the Lord was serious about keeping his word, the privilege of staying in scores of Christians' homes while doing tour ministries was the clinching proof.

A high school friend who loves the Lord and serves Him fully as a farm machinery manufacturer understands the ministry from the inside out. His parents are pastors. I was the first guest he and his wife had in their gorgeous hillside mansion overlooking a golf course. I love golf. It would have been easy for them to say, "We're not ready for company yet." The baseboards weren't on, the landscaping wasn't started, and there were a hundred and one little things left to finish. It would have been easy to say "no" to entertaining the missionary, but they didn't. They let me live with them for one fabulous week of rest and refreshing. I jogged on the golf course in the crisp morning air with the deer that make the woods their home. The trees were painted in extravagant fall tones. Those refreshing days on my native turf, just back from a hot bout with grassroots church planting in a steamy, dirty, third-world city, were like oil on my soul. I left renewed and ready for the six-week tour ahead. And as I walked out of the house, they said, not just politely but sincerely, "Whenever you're through you have a home. There'll be a motorized golf cart in the garage, and the green fees are taken care of." I believe them, and I'll be back! It is one of my "hundred homes."

We drove up the road a few miles to the next host home on the tour. The Shields live on a quiet country acreage on the lip of a sprawling valley. At the base of their property is the tow bar to a local ski slope. I love skiing. As I walked through the kitchen door Mrs. Shields said, not just politely but sincerely, "Make yourself at home. What's ours is yours!" I wanted to say, "I know, the Lord already told me," but I resisted. I was, however, catching on. One hundred homes! And when I left, it was with the Shields' full assurance that whenever we passed that way during ski season we had a home at the base of the ski run.

I could go on to tell you about other places, like a condo with a rooftop pool and fully equipped exercise room with a glorious view of the Toronto skyline, and within walking distance of a humungous shopping mall. I love working out in rooftop exercise rooms that have glorious views of the Toronto skyline! But I suspect you already know the story.

The lesson is clear. We cannot outgive God. We can trust Him with everything. . . even the untouchable things. We can trust Him with the loves of our lives. We will never be disappointed. We will never come out short. I can hardly wait to find out about the rest of my houses! If you are waging an internal battle over what it might cost you to commit to a short-term missions task, take heart! He CAN be trusted!

My Own Life

The last trust test is never totally over until we walk with the Lord through the final gate of human existence: Death itself. Brushes with death prepare us for it, but nothing can completely ready us for this final test. I have, however, had enough elementary lessons to assure you that we can trust Him with our life itself.

There are people who think this even if they don't say it: "You're throwing your life away". Questions like, "What is the attitude of the National Church to missionary presence?" suggest that my contribution in a foreign country may be wasted, or, at least, unappreciated. Others ask, "How long has the mission been working in your country?" The implication is somewhere there between the lines: "Haven't we been there long enough?" Sometimes the tone tells it all when attached to a question like, "What's it like to leave your kids here in college?" Others wonder out loud, "Have you ever thought about staying home till they get through school?" or "How old are your parents?

I am no martyr. I do what I do because I enjoy it. I have learned that, so far, I have not gone wrong by trusting my life to God. The principles are spiritual. The words of the song put it so well: "*It is in pardoning that we are pardoned, it is in giving that we receive, it is in dying we are born to eternal life.*"

When a young, enthusiastic, postwar college grad named Jim Elliott left behind the bright prospects of a career in America to give his life to the Auca Indians of the Napo River system in Ecuador, it was because he also believed his very life could be trusted to the Creator's hands. His classic college idealism was expressed in those unforgettable lines: "He is no fool who gives what he cannot keep to gain what he cannot lose." There is nothing foolish in trusting God with our very lives.

David called it the "valley of the shadow of death." I look at life's final chapter as something of a tunnel. I hate caves or tunnels, or for that matter anything dark and foreboding. You walk in and all you see is black and blacker. But there is something I have discovered about tunnels that I enjoy. As one penetrates the dark unknown and turns back to look at the entrance, light from the entrance reveals where you have walked, and gives perspective and shape and even color to what was once only impenetrable darkness. When I thought of tunnels in relationship to some of life's tough times, like a child going off to boarding school for the first time, or a parent saying goodbye to a child at the door of a dorm, it came out in verse.

The truth about tunnels, as you walk along,
It's only dark where you haven't gone.

When the Lord chooses to walk me through the last tunnel, I hope I can trust Him totally with my very life. Even though it will be new territory for me I hope I will walk through the tunnel with confidence knowing "the truth about tunnels", that as we walk along, "it's only dark where we haven't gone".

It was so dark, as we dropped down the mule trail to the river roaring below, I could not see where my feet were stepping. I chose to rivet my gaze on the splash of white on the shoulder of my companion who knew the trail. I did remember that up ahead the trail narrowed to a ledge along a rock cliff. Somehow, by watching the one ahead, we made it.

Others have gone ahead of us. Can we follow them as they followed Christ? In C. S. Lewis' *Chronicles of Narnia*, the children are lost in the forests of Narnia. Someone suggests he sees the shadow of Aslan the Lion. There are doubters, but because of the dark, they choose to follow the one who is following the shadow of the Lion. When we cannot trust fully, can we trust the ones who are following the form of the Lion?

Every relationship is built on trust. Are you living on the growing edge of the trust test? Is there some thing, little or large, some treasure the Lord is talking to you about trusting Him with? A selfish houseparent in another part of the world told of keeping some of her most precious books to herself by storing them in a cardboard box under her bed rather than putting them out where the little MK urchins could crumple, fold, mutilate, or otherwise destroy them. To her chagrin, one day she reached under the bed to enjoy the books she had hoarded, only to realize that an army of termites had done what she feared the children would. What she hoarded she lost to the termites. The ones she shared, she still had.

Does the Lord have access to everything? You CAN trust Him with your treasures. If a short or longer term commitment to His Kingdom's cause, in a cross-cultural context, is being short-circuited by a nagging concern that He might not quite be trusted with your affairs, or your life, let me assure you that He can be trusted with your treasures . . . the little things, the larger things, the loves of your life, and yes, even your life itself.

AN ORIENTATION EXERCISE

Practical Steps to Prepare for the Separations

1. Building Back-up Systems

A respected missionary mentor told me that when normal communication lines broke down between himself and his son, the game of tennis they had enjoyed for some time remained a communication back-up system that kept the relationship intact. One of the benefits of living at a distance from our children and family members has been the opportunity to build back-up systems of relating to them. Few fathers write letters to their teenagers to keep in touch. When I sensed I was missing out on spiritual input into my son's life during his senior year I started writing daily devotionals that I mailed to him. Those devotionals now form a value heritage that chronicles the special spiritual link that held my son and me together during those days. Writing to him helped me to keep a space open for him in my life. Prayer for my children always took on deeper dimensions when we were separated. Have a practical plan for building a back-up system of relating to significant people while you are separated. On a short trip, a daily journal entry will keep you linked emotionally to them, and when shared, will revitalize the relationship.

2. Redefining Home

Accepting a cross-cultural assignment means we will need to rework our definition of that comfort zone we call "home". Part of handling the separation-grief experiences of my lifestyle has been a healthy understanding of what home is. Early in our marriage, our wandering lifestyle led my wife to quip, "Home is where you hang your nightie." My daughter's wall in the house with the exotic flower planters was decorated with a little cross-stitch motto: "Home is where you hang your memories." While some MK's are embarrassed with the question, "Where's your home?," they are not necessarily sorry for such a lack in their life. They are simply uncomfortable with the expectation the question implies: that everyone should have a definite geographical place that is HOME. Even gypsies have their own definition of home.

Cross-cultural ministers are global nomads. There is a big difference between having no home, and learning to be comfortable with a different definition of what "home" is. Being away from the special people back home, even for a short time, may actually be an opportunity to enhance those "hearth bonds". You can often deepen a personal relationship through a daily journal, through correspondence, or through prayer.

The bottom line is that people who are willing to risk themselves in a short-term missions experience will have to redefine "home." Some may even have to sell their "homes" in order to go. When my parents made a mid-life course correction they lost an important peg on which we as a family had always hung our definition of "home." They gave up their postal box number. Something so seemingly insignificant left an emotional bruise on each member of the family. Although Mom and Dad retraced their steps to the old home roots again, a small but integral part of "home" was gone forever.

One thing is sure. There will always be bruises occasioned by the separations of cross-cultural ministry. Missions, short or long term, remains a contact sport.

Chapter 6

HOW TO LOOK AT ANOTHER CULTURE

THE FIRST THING WE DO when we enter a new world is to compare it with the only other one we know, our own. As a coordinator of short-term work groups I cringe at the prospect of turning loose a new team on the culture where I live as a guest. The total experience is invariably worth the pain, but in the process it is often necessary to deal with some rather premature judgments. It is very easy to confuse "what things are like" with "what things I like, or do not like." How can a visitor look perceptively into a new culture while avoiding premature comparisons?

WHAT TO DO WHEN YOU DON'T LIKE WHAT YOU SEE

Whenever we look closely at a culture we are bound to come to the conclusion that it could use some changes. This chapter is the first of three studies on what to do about affecting change in a culture. That, of course, is an arrogant assertion. Naturally many things in a new culture are different. But do any of them need changing? And who is to decide? Must I accept everything I see in a strange culture?

We need to begin by talking about the attractiveness of the Gospel in a trashy world. How can Christ's people can be agents to help put the color back into their own culture, or any other? The Apostle Paul did not back away from the anthropologists who argued cultural preservation at any cost. Some aspects of each culture are not worth keeping, and in fact require radical surgery if that society is to survive and prosper. It was so on the island of Crete that Paul visited. After looking around, he summarized what he saw and urged the resident pastor, Titus, to take definite action . . .

> *. . ."SO THAT IN EVERY WAY THEY WILL MAKE THE TEACHING ABOUT GOD OUR SAVIOR ATTRACTIVE."*
>
> Titus 2:10b

The people Paul refers to as "they" in v. 10b are slaves. He is telling them how to be Christian slaves in a sick society, that bred and fed on trade in human lives. The apostle believed that this "base" human being, according to the standards of Cretan culture, on the lowest rung of society, was capable of attractiveness, or of "adorning the Gospel" as another version puts it. We notice that the ugliness of slavery is not the first issue addressed. Change in Cretan culture would not come about by making sweeping cosmetic changes to something so symptomatic of that society as was the slave culture. Changing slavery in Crete for Titus was like Moses trying to resolve the individual problems of oppression for his people in Egypt. The solution was much deeper. God not only wanted to end slavery, He wanted to change the slaves themselves. It was easy to look at Crete and see slavery. Paul looked at Crete and saw the sin of the slaves as well.

I like to absorb the sights and sounds of the places where I serve. There is no better way to absorb life in a Latin American city than to sit down in one of the countless parks. Park life can be a reasonable facsimile of society. The parks in Guayaquil, Ecuador, where I worked for four years, are generally just big concrete pads where people congregate, wait for buses, and watch sidewalk sideshows of men swallowing swords, walking on glass or preaching hellfire. Most of the parks have statues, and a few have token trees. Even fewer have any grass, but all of them have plenty of people.

There are two important parks just three blocks apart in central Guayaquil. Centennial Park is the city's proud postcard image that sits squarely in the middle of the showcase street: Ninth of October Avenue. It's a symbol of what the city would like to look like. No buses are allowed on *Ninth of October* Avenue. No selling stalls or portable junk food vendors are permitted to set up their booths in this park. Here is where bands play, parades pass, and pictures are taken. It's the city's Sunday suit, so to speak.

Three blocks south of Centennial Park, bustling Victory Park attracts no tourists. There is nothing too attractive about Victory Park, but it is the vital nerve center of the city. It is what the city is! This is where working people make their connections from one city bus to another. Maids, bricklayers, students, shoppers and vendors line up at the end of the day in long, hot lines, waiting to pour into the bulging buses. A few desperate riders lunge for a final toe hold on the running board as the bus sprays its poisonous exhaust across the queue of people on the curb, already jostling for position on the next bus. A lady lofts a watermelon rind out a window. It grazes a passerby, who glares, and swears. The bus's choking fumes engulf a white-helmeted traffic policeman arguing with another driver about overloading his unit. There are orange peels in the gutter and political graffiti on the bandstand. It's not a pretty place, but when Christmas comes to Guayaquil it comes first to Victory Park. And it comes overnight.

One night, as dusk settles on the city, and as street sweepers clear the gutter of the regular residue of the after-work finger-food crowd, a transformation takes place. First, conspicuous piles of old boards appear, and plywood partitions begin to be raised. Battered tin roof sheeting is laid out over rickety rafters, and all around the park little shacks spring up. Overnight the park is transformed into a village of shops rimming the block. By morning the entire circumference is ringed with booth after booth of plastic toys, shimmering tinsel, and artificial Christmas trees. The next evening illegal wires are tossed up over the high tension lines and glittering colored bulbs accentuate the red and green tinfoil streamers, until the whole park is ablaze with light and color.

In a matter of hours, as if by magic, a greasy, grubby public spittoon of a place has been transformed into a shimmering, shiny princess of a park. We know that Christmas has come because a dusty grey park at the very heart of the city has been reborn.

The Christmas decorations in Victory Park help to remind me of what the Gospel of Christ will do in our world and in that world. They speak to me of the transformation of ordinary lives and less than attractive cultures into ornaments of God's grace.

> *. . ."so that in every way they will make the teaching about god our savior attractive. For the grace of God that brings salvation has appeared to all men."*
>
> Titus 2:10b

Christmas decorations don't change anything. Victory Park still has its smells and sweat. But Jesus Christ came to change ordinary people and cultures into ornaments of his grace.

HOW TO OBSERVE ANOTHER CULTURE

The apostle Paul was a keen observer of culture. We get the idea that he went out for a walk in the parks of Athens just to absorb the atmosphere. It says, "*he was greatly distressed to see the city was full of idols. . .*" and he comments later, "*As I walked around and observed your objects of worship. . .*"(Acts 17:16,23) When Paul looked, he saw deeply.

I have a colleague who so enjoys soaking up the smells and sounds of down-to-earth living in Latin culture that he goes to extremes. The last time he visited me in Guayaquil he went out for a walk in Centennial Park at seven in the evening. When he returned he was quieter than usual, but no one noticed, since "quiet" is quite usual for him. When he did talk, he croaked. Some crooks had put a choke hold on him in the park, lifted him in the air, and lifted his watch and documents from his pocket. Poking your nose into another culture can be risky business. Coincidentally, my friend's name is Paul.

The other Paul's walking tour of the island culture of Crete caused him to come to some frightful conclusions. This culture was not simply bad. It was hopeless. This culture not only needed an oil change, it needed a complete overhaul. *"Even one of their own prophets has said: 'Cretans are always liars, evil beasts, lazy gluttons.'"* (Titus 1:12)

That dangerous cultural generalization could have been taken as a racially charged slur had it not been cloaked in such a clever manner. *"Even one of their own prophets has said..."* The apostle had done his homework. He had read the local editorial page, attended a sidewalk theater performance, or sat in on a Cretan coffee shop conversation. "Don't take my word for it," he says. "This is what they say about themselves."

It's one thing to make vague cultural comparisons with our own world. It is something quite different to investigate and report what their own people say about themselves. *"Even one of their own prophets has said: 'Cretans are always liars, evil beasts, lazy gluttons.'"* The apostle might have gotten away with his prejudicial pronouncement if he had left well enough alone. Unfortunately Paul couldn't. In the very next verse he gives his personal opinion. *"This testimony is true,"* our missiological model blurts out. "I agree with their prophet," he says. "They ARE a lazy bunch of lascivious liars."

Most of us have formulated similar cultural stereotypes. Japanese are so gracious, Americans so aggressive, Canadians so cold, French so proud, British so stubborn, Jews so shrewd, and on and on! Cultural generalizations, both bad and good, are dangerous business. Our magnanimous overtures of approval ("what beautiful eyes they have", "they're all so friendly, so well dressed, so obliging") are often overridden by other generalizations ("they dump their garbage right in the street" or "they'll take advantage of you any chance they get").

For instance, I have discovered a law of human nature in Latin America as predictable as the famous Murphy's Law. It is another example of cultural generalization. It goes something like this: THE SUCCESS OF ANY VENTURE IS DIRECTLY PROPORTIONAL TO THE AMOUNT OF TIME YOU MUST STAND IN LINE FOR IT. In other words, no line is ever too long to stand in if you end up with what you came for.

Paul's observation of Cretan culture reminds me of two Chinese businessmen I overheard talking in a Quito airport lineup. All of a sudden, the line these oriental men were standing in broke down. *En masse*, the potential planeload of people stampeded the loading gate when they sensed that the flight had been overbooked. There were no seat assignments on domestic flights at the time. The two demure Chinese businessmen stood quietly in their places, briefcases in hand, where a line had once been, and the one commented to the other with perfect control: "What we have here is a DISTINCT lack of social discipline." (I could hear because I was still standing in line behind them trying to decide whether to be Chinese or Latin at the moment. Seconds later, I too charged the ticket counter!)

Some cultures are naturally more attractive than others. I admire Japanese neatness, German thoroughness, Swiss precision, and of course, Canadian reserve. A friend who visited us in Ecuador after a tour of Japan made an incredible appraisal of that people. "The Japanese people," he said, "are the most gracious, courteous and generous people I have ever seen." His three superlatives bowled me over. I have no reason to doubt him. But what to do with cultures that are not quite so appealing?

I took a break while writing this chapter to take my son to the soccer field. On the way we drove past *Fundación Natura*, the Ecuadorian environmental watchdog organization charged with the frightful task of educating and policing environmental control in this developing nation. Right there at the curb in front of the *Fundación Natura* offices was a bus driver changing his oil and filter. A massive pool of black oil glinted on the asphalt under his bus and the old filters were abandoned on the sidewalk. Something inside me revolts. Is there any hope? Signs in local buses used to read: "Don't be a pig. Throw your garbage out the window."

Gratefully cultures can change. When a taxi driver emptied the garbage from his last client in front of my house I pointed it out and he promptly gathered it up. A teenager from the church tossed a candy wrapper in the gutter outside after a service. The street was already helplessly swimming with garbage. When I mentioned it, kindly, he was embarrassed, and bent down to pick it up. Yet, is this my role? What aspects of a culture really need to be changed? When can I feel free to correct? And deeper inside is the nagging question, "What is correct?"

Paul left Titus in the middle of a culture whose characteristics were less than admirable. His assessment was that they needed considerable work. "*ALWAYS liars, evil beasts, lazy gluttons.*" If there was something good about this people, Paul did not bother to mention it. There was, in Paul's eyes, little to recommend. Yet what does the apostle say? "This is a cultural write off?" "I'm sending you to the next island where the people are nicer?" Not on your life!

The apostle uses his evaluation of the islanders as a basis for the kind of ministry Titus is to have. He will need to approach them in a specific way BECAUSE OF who they are.

The "Therefore" of verse 13 is a tremendous semantic bridge. Having made his radical cultural observations he goes on to make some missiological applications. He proceeds to tell Titus how to deal with these people. People who are "*always liars, evil beasts, lazy gluttons*" require special attention. "*Rebuke them sharply.*" A firm hand is advised. The three short chapters are riddled with words like "*teach,*" "*train,*" "*encourage*" and "*remind*". Titus' task would be heavy on education, making Biblical links to a delinquent culture.

Having seen what there is to see, can we build the bridge to doing what there is to do about it? Paul's goal for Titus' ministry was that when he left, everybody from the housewives to the slaves, would be walking, living advertisements of the beauty of the Gospel of Christ.

> *". . . So that in every way they will make the teaching about God our Savior attractive. For the grace of God that brings salvation has appeared to all men."(Even Cretans, Paul would say.)*

Back Home Blues

One of the side benefits of going abroad is being able to see your own culture more clearly. When I go home to Canada people invariably ask, "What's it like to be back?" Naturally it was good to be back but things had changed. 200,000 Canadians were now into "rec" hockey (a game on ice for old wrecks). It had barely been invented when I left for the mission field. Had I stayed in Canada I would have been one more of those old wrecks rattling around some rink on the weekend. Now I can look at a cultural phenomenon from a more detached stance.

A colleague made the comment on coming back home, "All the people seem so pale." After a term among the richer skin tones of South America, North Americans seemed pale. A culture can lose its color, as well. Values can blur, causes can dim, and the "issues of the day" for those who have been away for awhile seem somewhat pale.

I noticed back home that everybody wanted a new day in court. Families of WW II victims were seeking settlements. In Boston an organization under the name of "Sons and Daughters of the Victims of Colonial Witch Trials" was seeking to revive their cause 300 years after the events. The preoccupation with personal rights is not seen as clearly till you spend time in a culture where rights are related to muscle and money.

As a short-term visitor the opportunity to affect change in the host culture will be minimal. It would probably be unwise to try. The first and hardest step to being a change agent is to quietly observe. However, the return to your native culture will afford opportunities to see things you have never quite seen before, and to begin to be a change agent for Christ in your own world. The greatest benefit of a trip abroad may be the new insights you glean on how to live challengingly at home.

Orientation Planning: TRIP TIP

Paul took a walk around Athens and then strolled the streets of Crete. What did he watch for? Here's a start-up checklist on how to look at another culture.

- ❑ Step inside a hardware store and study how people find clerks, choose items, make purchases and receive their merchandise. Don't be in a hurry!
- ❑ Ride a complete bus circuit observing: how to pay, how to stop the bus from inside, from outside, how people relate to each other, what is the attitude toward women, children, and the elderly.
- ❑ Stand on a busy corner or public park for a full two hours and write down everything you see, including how the shoe shine boy signals to his clients.
- ❑ Sit in a cathedral for at least an hour and study faces, gestures and attitudes. Who comes, What did they come for, and how did they leave?
- ❑ Visit a government office where there is heavy paperwork traffic. Sit in the main waiting room and try to figure out the system. Who goes where to get what done?
- ❑ Spend an afternoon wandering the city's bus terminal till you understand the way it works.
- ❑ Watch a policeman at work on a busy corner for at least an hour.

For each of these items, watch for five minutes, write down your observations, then watch another 35 minutes to see how your perceptions change. The point is to look long enough to see! And as you watch another world unfold before you, make note of the positive features you would wish to transport back home with you.

Chapter 7

WHAT TO SEE IN ANOTHER CULTURE

THE KEY TO UNDERSTANDING another culture is looking long enough till you start to see. Concentrated observation at a single location will do more to give you an accurate glimpse of another culture than twenty whirlwind guided tours, during which you are always stopped at just the right spot to take pictures, and the tour group comes home with twenty photos of the same thing.

I have learned this lesson the hard way. A vehicle fails on an isolated road. You take a bus back to the nearest town, hire a heavy truck to tow you in, and spend an afternoon bumming around a mechanic shop in a two-bit town while the experts do the work. What is there to do? Sit and watch people. Or the road is closed ahead because of a landslide, so you sit in a line of traffic for four or five hours and watch the world come and go.

Traveling in rural Ecuador I soon learned that when you are offered a seat on the board bench under the porch roof of a farmer's home you are visiting, and no one stays to visit with you, you can be sure you will be there awhile. Everyone is busy preparing your welcome meal. You can confirm that suspicion by watching the dogs round up the chicken. Some of my best lessons have been learned watching the world go by while waiting for the rooster to boil.

I am an impatient learner. I do not do these things voluntarily. Yet, after twenty years in Latin America, enough of them have "happened to me" to give me a cross section of life here. The casual visitor may have to deliberately stage some such extended study sessions if he wants to really SEE the culture.

Seeing with your Ears

One morning in my first term I was assaulted by the incredible invasion of sounds around me. I recorded what I heard and the morning sounded something like this:

MORNING SOUNDS

The first truck of the day belches its way to work disturbing the silence of the streets. An upstaged rooster behind a mud-wall barrier registers a vain protest against this rude incursion of big-city sounds on his private and personal domain. But it is too late. The city is already awake.

A chorus of dog barks ricochets through the valley, and like a wave breaking on the beach, sweeps back over the city again. A steel wheel on pavement crunches to a halt as the street sweeper pauses below the window to make a playful swish at the remains of last night's garbage pickup.

A raucous stereo reverberates through the halls and off the concrete walls of a neighbor's house, a full dozen decibels on the high side of tolerance. A passing whistler struggles to accompany the music.

Away and below a carpenter's saw groans an aching complaint as it bends its back to the day's duties. Beyond, a hammer rattles its first tentative taps on a crumpled fender, grim reminder of somebody's Saturday.

The rooster rebukes the roar of another truck, and a car horn aimed at nothing in particular careens through an empty intersection.

Now there are voices on the sidewalk, the clack of heels, the staccato of motorcycles and the throaty grumbling of buses burdened with bodies. There is less conversation and more traffic as the morning ripens and the city settles into the serious hum of another day.

Only the occasional cackle of a hen heralding the day's production, or the distant moo of a cow on its way to market unseats the urbanness of it all, and reminds us that this is still a city struggling to be one. There are bursts of silence, temptingly rural, then a barrage of noise when the entire gamut of sounds assaults the ear and creates a confusing cacophony of city and country.

The girl's school rector rages in quadraphonic at some minor infraction of the rules. The broom boy wails the virtues of his wares. A radio somewhere blares the deal of the day. The tap of tools is more insistent. And the rooster crows on indignantly. No one hears him now.

It is very possible to see things in another culture by just listening for them. Perhaps a tape recorder would work just as well, but the point is, each sound has a whole world of meaning behind it. Tune your ear as well as your eye!

Seeing with your Mind

Anyone with an elemental eye for observation can spot the differences between one culture or another. It is making sense of the differences and being able to intelligently express those differences that adds the essential third dimension to our observation. It takes serious thought to make sense of what you see, so that you come out of the experience with more than a travelogue that says, "things are sure different there."

What does a soccer stadium and cemetery have in common? The stratification of society in Latin America had always intrigued me but it wasn't until I saw the similarities between the soccer stadium and the cemetery that the phenomenon came together for me.

Most of the stadium seating consisted of concentric concrete circles of benches without backs. Another quarter of the stadium was dedicated to individual aluminum seats, and the remaining ten percent was reserved for plush box-seat compartments. It struck me that the individual seats, a rather new innovation in South American soccer stadiums, suited the lifestyle of the dentist who had invited me to the game. He was solidly middle class. The style of seating he had chosen reflected the new reality of the emerging middle class in Latin America. The stadium seating arrangement was actually a microcosm of the stratification of society.

In the cemetery the social differences are evident. Elaborate mausoleums provide resting places for the remains of all the members of a single wealthy family. Just as the upper class crowd looks down from the luxury of their private suites on the masses crammed on concrete benches at the soccer stadium, the same social grouping creates private burial chapels to isolate themselves even when life is over. The poor are shelved away in above-ground concrete filing cabinet structures, or they scratch out a hole in the ground high up on cemetery hill. As at the stadium, in the cemetery a new class of construction, almost like a high-rise building, was appearing. The emerging middle class was calling for a new kind of burial ground as well. Viewing the cemetery and soccer stadium as a microcosm of a class-conscious culture was an important clue to understanding the culture.

Serious study of a culture heightens one's consciousness of its spiritual need. When I reflected on the city of Guayaquil, to which I had been assigned, and the spiritual fate of its two million inhabitants, I was impressed by the daily scene on the city's main artery. During the five o'clock rush, traffic is actually diverted off the fast lanes of Quito Street so that funeral processions on foot can have priority on the way to the cemetery. As I meditated on the city, and the irony of fast-lane funeral traffic, I tried to put my feelings into verse.

People up and going,
but I'm not too certain where.
Life looks a bit disheveled,
but we're not supposed to stare.
Do they know where they are going?
It all seems so prearranged.
Through the struggle for survival
nothing ever seems to change.
What makes things so uneven?
You can't say this thing is fair.
Who makes the rules we live by?
Doesn't anybody care?
Just a number on a tombstone,
An empty window on a wall,
Just a corner in the market,
When he's gone who'll get the stall?
I wonder is that all?
People up and going,
could you point him to the road?
Would you help him with his load?
People up and going,
Soon he'll be across the river.
Does he know that it's forever?
Here today, and gone tomorrow.
Life so short, the end so final.

Whether by means of verse, sketch, or contemplative photography, thorough thinking must go into your observation of the culture. Seeing a culture with your mind can sensitize you to the deeper issues of their existence if you are prepared to pay the price of serious observation.

Seeing Through Yourself

A wise Creator gave us two eyes. That provides depth perception. The only way to obtain an adequate depth perception in viewing a foreign culture is to keep both eyes wide open. By keeping one eye on ourselves as we look at others we can gain valuable perspective on both cultures. As I become more aware of how I am seen I am able to understand some of the "why" of the new culture. From my limited experience in orienting people on how to act in a different culture I have found the following profile helpful in avoiding early errors.

Richard P. Reichert

A North American Profile

The way we view
ourselves may not be
how others see us.

1. Private or Proud

We may have no fences around our front lawns but there are very real invisible fences around us and our possessions. The North American person's sense of privacy is perceived as very proud because we wall our self in and won't let anyone into our world. People will overcrowd buses or benches, and we may feel that no one else can fit, but another one or two or three will squeeze in, often encroaching on our invisible fence. As we stand in line or walk down the street, it is good to remember that we are on their turf.

What constitutes getting cut off in traffic is quite relative depending on the culture you are in. A North American driver expects to be allowed several car lengths before a vehicle can come into his lane. In other parts of the world just getting your nose ahead of the car beside you, gives you the right to cut in. There are unwritten codes of space in every culture.

People may come too close when they talk. If you draw back, your sense of privacy may be viewed as pride, regardless of your reasons.

May I sit with you?
"No the bench is already full."
May I see your hotel room?
" And let you see all the things I have?"
May I carry your camera?
"Are you kidding? It cost me $400."

2. Observant or Snoopy

The typical North American tourist is quite inquisitive. He is always poking his camera into some hidden or forbidden spot. The questioning mind is a commendable characteristic of our upbringing. Yet, that value in our culture can be a liability elsewhere. Our self confidence can come across as being snoopy. Our need to understand will be seen by some as being pushy. While we want to be thorough in exploring their world, it is wise to opt for a casual brand of curiosity.

3. Productive or Impersonal

It is hard for missions work teams to realize that they have come primarily not to do projects but to meet people. Despite the obvious agenda of building a latrine, or painting a seminary on a two-week time line, it is essential to never let what you are doing get in the way of the people around. It may be much more important to leave a wall undone or a board uncut in order to be sensitive to the people around you. North American project-minded people are often considered impersonal or impatient because of their production mentality. Action-oriented, energy-efficient, goal-driven people find it hardest to fit in to a short-term working visit and often leave frustrated and unfulfilled.

One work group I supervised was distraught that the jungle church they had envisioned building and dedicating in two weeks did not look much different after they had come and gone. The "before and after" picture was a dismal failure. Another work team wilted in the jungle heat and made themselves sick trying to maintain a western work ethic in a tropical setting, hauling rocks from the river in jute sacks strapped over their foreheads. Although our work group quit at four in the afternoon, some who lived in that Indian culture commented: "This is the longest our people have ever worked in a single day." The Indians had more sense than to work in the hot sun. Abandoning a pre-planned agenda can be one of the most excruciating lessons of short-term cross-cultural interchange.

4. Well- Equipped Or Materialistic

The average North American tourist tends to be over equipped and under aware. Having everything on hand that is needed for a trip or a work project can give the appearance that you are "filthy rich." While having enough tape measures, brushes, and scrapers for everyone on the project makes efficiency-sense to us, we often come across as cluttered collectors. It is not uncommon for construction workers to share hammers. Keep a low profile on your possessions. First, it may be the best way to ensure that you will still have them when you leave. But more importantly, your image as worshippers of the god of the gadget has preceded you. Try to change that image by living as simply as possible. In much of Latin America it is culturally insensitive to flash cash in public. And watch out for waste. Playing with food, or paint, may seem like innocent fun to us. To others it may look like we are flaunting our wealth.

5. Discriminating or Fussy

What to me may be a very good sense of taste may actually be in bad taste. We come from a land of plenty where 31 flavors of Baskin Robbins may not be enough. We have come to a land of poverty where having anything at all is more than enough. In some restaurants in my adopted home of Ecuador there are no menus. It is simply breakfast, dinner and supper. You do not need to bother asking what's for dinner. Just ask is there dinner?

I cringe when taking tour groups shopping, watching them compare the quality of workmanship of the artisan who is standing behind the counter. Unwittingly, by pointing out small defects of color, shade or texture, they make a social statement about inferiority, not of the craft, but of the person. Work teams usually marvel when they send me to buy more screws of a particular size, or head-type, and I return with just plain "screws." I was raised on the Sears catalogue categories of Good-Better-Best, and I like comparison shopping as much as most people. Time and a dozen disappointments, however, have tempered that keen eye for the "right screw."

In the end, it is just a matter of perspective, as a Costa Rican craftsman taught me early in our career. My wife and I saw some candle holders that caught our eye. On closer scrutiny we were sorry to see that each candle holder, though the identical model, had a mark that distinguished it from the other. We were looking for a matched pair, and registered our protest with the shop owner. "How can you expect to sell candle holders that are not in matching pairs?" To which the unflappable merchant replied, "Of course they are not in pairs. Each one is *muy exclusivo.*" (very exclusive) What I had seen as a glaring defect in his product he deftly transformed into an obvious virtue. Since that day when we are frustrated by a dozen eggs that are all shapes and colors, or a set of wall hangings clearly intended to be a set but anything but identical, my wife and I like to remind ourselves how fortunate we are that each egg or wall hanging is *"muy exclusivo."*

We have been raised to believe that we have rights and choices. Being accustomed to personal preferences can be a disadvantage. Our hosts may see that as being picky. Forget about your commitment to fat-free diets, to health foods and to certain favorite eating styles as you travel and visit in other parts. Drink coffee when you are offered it, without wondering whether it's "decaf" or not. The concept of "decaf" or "diet" may not have caught on where you happen to be going. It is not in good taste to take it upon yourself to convince your hosts of the merits. Your "discretion" only distresses a host trying desperately to please and you present the image of a finicky, picky or fussy individual.

6. Punctual or Inflexible

If there is one virtue that many Latinos begrudgingly admire in North Americans, it is our insistence on being on time. Ecuadorians make nervous fun of their tendency toward tardiness, or the *"hora ecuatoriana,"* as they themselves refer to it. Yet, at the same time, they view our clock-punching as inflexible and unfeeling. We come across as over-organized. Don't rush away from people because "it's time to go." It's never "time to go" until all the good-byes have been properly attended to.

"Then when the usher gives the signal you have exactly 45 seconds for your prayer before the choir director cuts you off."

Profile Of The Host Culture

In analyzing any culture it is a valuable exercise to convert what I consider to be a weakness into strength by asking the question, "How can that action or attitude be expressed in a positive way?" As an example, let me illustrate from the Latin culture I am beginning to appreciate. There is a stereotype that says Latinos tend to be "lazy, undisciplined and emotional." It's a lie! What some may seem as laziness is just a relaxed, easygoing lifestyle. What may appear to be a lack of discipline is really spontaneous creativity. What seems like hotheadedness or sentimentality is one of the highest virtues of Latin culture: deeply sensitive people.

Just as it is important to remember how one as a North American is perceived, it is wise to have a head start as to what to anticipate about the host culture. For example, if you are privileged to travel in South or Central America here are four virtues that seem to stand out. They may equally apply to other non-North American cultures.

1. The Importance Of People

Greeting is an essential ritual. Walking past a person without greeting is unpardonable. Don't ever walk away from the circle of a conversation without excusing yourself with a nod, a handshake or a word. A heavy overdose of handshaking is always acceptable. Good-byes are expected. Farewells are an unavoidable formality.

2. The Tentativeness Of Trust

You are being evaluated and judged for all North Americans and what they have said or done, or are supposed to be like. A backlog of bad experiences and political propaganda is weighted against the prospect of gaining instant respect in their world. Earning trust is a long-range road and a highly prized attainment in any relationship. The brash North American can storm into a setting and feel he has won the confidence of the group in a matter of minutes. They will tell you when they trust you. Don't assume it until they do!

3. The Need For Acceptance

Your hosts are hungry for compliments about their country and culture. There is an inbred sense of insecurity and a feeling of inferiority among developing cultures that we do not understand. We may look at them as equal but in their mind they know, or believe, they are not. We can unconsciously feed that feeling of inferiority by parading our possessions, making innocent comparisons between our country and theirs, asking for more of this or that, not eating this or that, or just speaking in English in the presence of others who do not understand.

4. The Instinct For Adaptability

Try to appreciate the tremendous spirit of innovation that keeps some third world cultures running. I have heard local journalists boast of being world champions of improvisation. Admire the ability to make do with things we would throw out. Remember, they can't afford to throw it out. What seems to us like a lack of planning is really one of the most adventurous aspects of life in Latin America. You never know what may happen next. So just and relax and go with the flow!

Seeing the flipside of what we consider cultural quirks adds depth and perspective to our appreciation of a new culture. Opposites do actually attract! There is something ingenious about being impromptu after all, and something breath-takingly creative about waiting till the last minute.

Seeing A Culture As God Sees It

The most valuable way of seeing another culture is by putting the divine microscope of the Word to work. When Isaiah looked at the society of his day he observed that it was sick to the core. It was rotten at its roots. The very things the prophet predicted would be affected by the disobedience of Israel as a nation are affected today by spiritual indifference.

> *"The Lord Almighty is about to take from Jerusalem and Judah both supply and support. All supplies of food and water, the hero and warrior, the judge and prophet, the soothsayer and elder, the captain of fifty and man of rank, the counselor, skilled craftsman and clever enchanter."*
>
> Isaiah 3:1-3

When a society is sick spiritually, sustenance and basic services suffer. National defense loses its luster. Spiritual resources wither. The judicial support system fails. The educational system is ineffective. Technical prowess is stifled. The idea mill shrivels.

Once these principal props of a people are threatened, they are ripe for revolution. If you want to see a society the way God does, take a look at these basic elements. As you visit a new culture, find solid answers to these key questions:

1. Who controls the food supply and basic services? In what condition are they?
2. Does the military superstructure serve society or operate in isolation from it? How do you get ahead in the armed forces?
3. What are the spiritual resources of this culture? Are they adequate? What alternates are on the horizon?
4. Does the judicial system work for everyone? What is the legal process like?
5. Do you understand the school system? What are the options for young people in education in this culture? Have you visited the main centers of learning for a morning?

This kind of deeper study of a society presupposes time and some language skill but for the keen short-termer there are shortcuts. Pre-reading is helpful and English-speaking nationals can be found. A good picture of a culture can be gained by investigating these crucial areas.

Nothing eats at me like the corruption I see in the essential services and government agencies established to alleviate the suffering of the people they serve. The cannibalistic nature of a sin-riddled society is sickening. *"People will oppress each other—man against man, neighbor against neighbor."* (Isaiah 3:5) There is something cannibalistic about every culture, the tendency to turn in on and devour itself. That was what had happened in Israel. *"The young will rise up against the old, the base against the noble,"* he says.

> *"The Lord enters into judgment against the elders and leaders of his people: 'It is you who have ruined my vineyard; the plunder of the poor is in your houses. What do you mean by crushing my people and grinding the faces of the poor?'"*
>
> Isaiah 3:14,15

A cross cultural experience that skims the surface of these real issues is not worth the investment. Look deep enough to see the real issues.

Special Redemptive Clues

There is something else to watch for as you observe and analyze other cultures. Among some peoples, the Almighty has concealed redemptive clues that can help them understand and come to Christ. Don Richardson's discovery of the "Peace Child" as a type of Christ that unlocked the spiritual destiny of an entire people is the classic example. Other less spectacular clues may be found to help a specific people understand and accept Jesus Christ as the Universal Savior.

Washington Leon, founder of an Ecuadorian mission agency, feels that among the Shuar of southern Ecuador the "dance of the snake" holds potential to reach this unreached people. In the legend, a man bitten by a snake is touched by the pinchers of a river crab. The crab is then thrown into the water to go and tell the snake that his bite has been ineffective. The good news for Shuar people is that the Serpent's bite is indeed ineffective and that healing and eternal life have been won by the Christ who has crushed the Serpent's head.

High over Quito towers the impressive statue of the Virgin Mary standing on a great globe. The statue honors Mary as the constitutional queen of Ecuador. There is a gigantic ugly snake at her feet, but the snake is tied loosely to Mary by a chain held delicately in her fingers. There is no sign of the titanic struggle between good and evil, between Christ and Satan, as presented in Genesis 3:15. The monument, visited by thousands, is a travesty to the truth of that Scripture. It was the seed of the woman who would crush the snake (inflict a mortal wound), though that snake would bruise His heel (inflict a temporary blow).

The tourists who dutifully trek to the top of the Panecillo hill where the statue stands, merely to snap a picture of this domesticated devil, and go home to show their friends the "statue that overlooks the city," have looked but have not seen. The truly Christian visitor who comes to "see" the culture will not miss these spiritual lessons. To a people crushed by corruption, pursued by poverty, and lacerated by lies, this statue stands as testimony to the failed religious resources and flawed social system over which the statue stands a mute and powerless guardian. To look at the statue and not see the spiritual implications over which the sentinel stands is perhaps the larger crime. Instead, turn your tourism into a prayer walk. Wherever your camera and your curiosity take you as you explore a new and different culture, may Mike Otto's lyrics be your personal prayer: "*Let me see this world oh Lord, as though looking through your eyes.*" Then, and only then, will you really see anything.

AN ORIENTATION EXERCISE FOR TEAM LEADERS

As your prepare to be as inconspicuous as a foreigner can be, consider these scenarios and suggestions for you or your team.

1. Travelling on a public bus, the driver takes a break on the side of the road. The male passengers get out and stand in a line along the road side in order to:

- ❑ see the sights
- ❑ stretch their legs
- ❑ offer a group prayer for protection
- ❑ answer the call of nature

How private a person are you? Are you ready to forgo your normal standards of propriety and privacy in order to fit in?

2. Design a group dynamic or project where there are deliberately not enough pencils, saws or scissors to go around. See how people handle the frustration of "not enough" and discuss the reactions. Decide what equipment you can share. Would you consider a designated cameraman for the day so that everyone in the group does not appear with a camera?

3. The church women bring a refreshing strange concoction to the work site. There are 5 glasses and fifteen of you. They have a suspicious-looking pail of water along and dip the glass halfheartedly in the bucket after each person has had his drink. To not drink is to commit an unpardonable social offense. At an orientation lunch serve only one kind of coke (not diet), and make sure there are not enough glasses to go around.

4. Come late to an orientation exercise. Wait till people get nervous or start to leave before you enter. Leave again to get your Bible. Talk about how you will handle "inefficiency" traps and delays."

Chapter 8

HOW TO ACT IN ANOTHER CULTURE

THE GOAL OF CROSS-CULTURAL MINISTRY is not contact, but impact. Sometimes it is easy to convince ourselves that because we have made meaningful contact with another culture, we have accomplished something. Understanding another culture is only the foundation to making an impact. It is a giant step from contact to impact. Impact implies change. One of the touchstones of being an agent for change is the skill of being confrontational within the acceptable norms of a society.

Energy levels were high. After a six hour drive through the dust to Buena Esperanza, the youth evangelism team had just had a refreshing swim in the creek and finished off their chicken dinner. It was time to get to work. Franco aimed the portable sound system up into the hills as the sun set over the mountain. "Come on down and enjoy the program," he called into the microphone. For people in those parts, visitors from the city were rare. "Special music," he tantalized, "testimonies, singing, preaching!" Something must have been missing. "And an exciting gospel film," he added for emphasis. That was bound to bring them. I was standing right next to him when he said it, and almost dropped my teeth. Franco knew that we had not brought the projector because there was no room for the heavy generator. He knew there were no films, but he could not resist the temptation to fill the little chapel by promising them what he couldn't deliver. I called him aside. "Brother Franco, that is a lie. You know there will be no film."

His head dropped. He was embarrassed. Later, Franco would thank me for calling his attention to his conduct. Today Franco and I are good friends.

The national pastor called on me in my home office one day, unexpectedly. The room was a mess and the desk a disaster. "Please pardon the mess," I offered. "Brother Richard," he retorted in his usually crisp manner, "You don't need to apologize for the mess. You need to clean up your desk." It was my turn to be embarrassed. I have never forgotten his mild rebuke, and I always think twice before apologizing for something I could or should have done.

A colleague of mine gave a seminary Christian Ethics exam in which considerable cheating by copying occurred. The professor chose to negate the results, to the protests of her pupils. An alternate exam was given in which two different versions were handed out so no one could copy from his neighbor. Some in the class cried "foul play" and refused to write it. The frustrated teacher was forced to prepare a third version of the exam for the dissenters.

As a seminary professor among both Spanish and Quichua cultures, the issue of giving an exam to my students has made me alternately angry, sad, frustrated and even vengeful. In a culture where copying is the norm and there is no clear linguistic equivalent for "cheating," I confess to having let things slide rather than constantly policing what seems like a lost cause. The difficulty in determining what to do when they cheat has even driven me to opt out of certain teaching situations because of the emotional tensions this dilemma has produced.

Among the students of the Indian institutes, I have discovered a very different dynamic at work than the sneakiness of some of my Spanish students. The Quichua students do not disguise their copying. In fact they try to help each other. While a student may know all the answers, and have finished the test, he will remain in his seat until all are finished. Writing an exam, like any other activity among them, is first and foremost a community project.

Just as they would not think of letting a member of the commune struggle to build a house without helping, they could not conceive of letting him struggle over a test paper without sharing what they know to help him finish. After a few feeble attempts to isolate people physically, I began to sense the tension so strongly in the room that I decided to allow them to help each other, give take-home exams, and emphasize group evaluation rather than individual academic competition. The result has been a more relaxed classroom and greater rapport with the students.

The above illustrations are shared to indicate how sensitive is the matter of daring to confront people of another culture about behavioral norms. Have I earned the right to confront their conduct? If I take personal offense at an exam-copying experience, I have lost the battle. "What to do when they cheat? " is the wrong question. "What is cheating, and do they know what it is?" is a saner approach.

Changes That Matter

I must continually remind myself that some changes I might want to make in a culture are not worth going to war over. I deliberately backed up traffic five or six cars by insisting on staying in the "proper" lane, forcing the man trying to turn in front of me to lose face and back off. The more culturally correct action would have been some creative, though not totally legal, maneuver in order for every one to be able to leave the scene happy. Sometimes our stubborn ego obnoxiously gets in the way, and we try to force minor changes that in the end will make little difference to anyone.

Correcting the way people drive is a prime example. While there are some international traffic norms that make driving in Latin America look vaguely familiar, one is not to be fooled by appearances. Traffic laws are not inviolable rules, but are taken more as suggested guidelines, to be adapted to the contingencies of the moment. The key question is, "What causes are worth fighting for?"

Changes That Last

On a church construction project in the isolated rural town of Orianga, a short-term team helped me construct the first outhouse in town. The town tradition was to head off into the banana groves whenever nature called. My wife refused to accompany us on the project if we didn't do something about that basic inconvenience. The group celebrated the completion of the prefab unit by staging an official inaugural sit-in. The wooden structure lasted about the length of the construction project; and then the humid weather took over and it rotted on the spot.

On a future visit to inaugurate the finished church building we were pleasantly surprised to find that more than one family in the town had constructed a brick version of our prototype. Without forcing on anyone a different lifestyle, change took place. I can imagine the housewives of the town chatting with their husbands at night about the advantages of the idea until the concept of brick "biffies" caught on and real lasting change took place in a culture.

"You DID say
'make disciples'
didn't you Lord?"

Acting Or Reacting

As in all of life, it is important to act, not to react. My five year old daughter Jennifer used to go through the open market with her fingers clamped on her nose. "It stinks," was her unapologetic excuse. There are some things about any culture that just plain "stink."

The varying manifestations of *machismo* stink in whatever culture or context they appear. At a recent home discipleship cell, Mariana confessed to a root of bitterness that had been growing in her marriage for months. Her elderly grandmother was failing and arrangements were made to go for a visit. Mariana's husband, like many men, grumbled about having to baby-sit for the day and make his own meals, but reluctantly agreed to let her go. Mariana got ready. The next morning, as the car arrived at the door to take her, Mariana's husband suddenly reversed his decision. She could not go. Late that weekend, Mariana's grandmother died. The two had been very close. Mariana's husband never spoke again of the incident, but boiling inside Mariana was a deep distrust for her husband that bordered on hate. Must the arbitrary authority of *machismo* be accepted as part of the culture, or dare I confront that undesirable norm?

My children play the tunnel game with a little more feeling than North American kids—trying to hold their breath till the car exits the tunnel. The tunnels in Quito are thick with car fumes. There is no ventilation. It gives added motivation to keep your nose plugged till you clear the tunnel.

There are missionaries who take forays into the culture then come back, almost literally holding their breath. When my wife or I return to the house drained by some brush with the culture and in need of being soothed, we announce, "I just had a cultural experience." It is a signal to the other that the one has been pushed to the tolerance level for the day and feels the need for retreat and an emotional stroke. A "cultural experience" can be a long lineup, a fouled up bank operation, an unreasonable sales clerk, or a rude taxi driver.

My wife was driving along a major thoroughfare when a young fellow galloped a horse right out in front of her, breaking the mirror and denting the door. When she tried to protest the carelessness, a taxi driver intervened: "You didn't expect the horse to put on his brakes, did you?"

How to Counter a Corrupt Culture

Sunder Krishnan makes a pastoral plea for the Canadian congregation to whom he ministers to practice counter cultural living, by which he means "resisting the pressure of the surrounding culture."[2] Titus' encounter with the Cretan culture models the same solution to a culture that "stinks." You only combat evil with good, lying with telling the truth, stealing with sharing, consumerism with moderation, laziness with work, and rebelliousness with subjection to authority. Whatever is bad needs to be balanced by doing "*whatever is good.*" Paul told Titus in Titus 3:1:

[2] Sunder Krishnan. *World Christians: Living on the Wavelength of the Great Commission.* Welch Publishing Co. Burlington: Ontario. 1989. p.71.

> *"Remind the people to . . . do whatever is good."" Our people must learn to devote themselves to doing what is good."*
>
> Titus 3:14

The apostle's advice to Titus is that a culture characterized by people who are "always liars, evil beasts, lazy gluttons" needs clear counter cultural models. The Cretan Christians are to be reminded to "*do whatever is good.*" Paul's own ministry team "*must learn to devote themselves to doing what is good.*" The salt of goodness on a society of badness will always have an effect.

Short-term visitors will not have as many opportunities as career missionaries, to effect change through confrontational Bible teaching, but they can be sowers of a counter cultural lifestyle that reinforces Scripture with confrontational Bible living. There are many things we'd like to change, but can't. Still, every public appearance in a culture is another opportunity to influence change by your example.

There are two surefire ways to be salt in a strange society no matter how short your stay.

1. Show consistent Christian character in the face of difficulty.
2. Show persistent love for the people regardless of differences.

Consistent Character

I walked with a visiting tour group through one of those dark "cultural experiences" you hope will never happen to your guests. One day before returning home after a full three-country tour, they were treating us to a pleasant Sunday dinner at a restaurant that straddles the equator. The meal was delicious and spirits were high, that is until they boarded the contracted tour bus to go back to the hotel. The bus had been left unattended by the tour company, and thieves had broken into the bus. Because they had been promised that their things would be safe inside, souvenir leather jackets, cameras, a passport and a valuable diary chronicling their entire trip had been left inside. They were gone.

No amount of badgering the driver could bring things back. I observed anger, which is natural; but I also saw the Christian grace of acceptance seeping through to quell the seething inside and bring calm. Here were people, most of whom could not speak enough Spanish to scream "robber," demonstrating the spiritual power of overcoming evil by good through their example of Christian character under adversity. The setbacks that face short-term visitors can be anything from robberies to lost luggage, to schedule changes, to missed flights, to diarrhea.

Persistent Love

Ted (I'll call him Ted) was the typical obnoxious tourist type: Too loud in the bus, too late for his Youth Corps team meetings, too lazy to help with the luggage, too large to fit in any public transit seat the country offered, and too fussy to fit the restricted menus of the frustrated missionaries. But Ted had come to see and to serve. He did not pound nails nearly as well as his fellow team members. He did not play any instruments and he certainly could not sing. About all Ted did was make friends with the kids. He loved them, and they loved him. When I go back to the town where his team worked, they do not ask about Rory, who could sling concrete with the best of the men, nor do they ask for Alice, who was bilingual and gave a stirring farewell charge. They do not even ask for Andrea, who could play her flute like an angel. When I go back to the town they are always asking for Ted, who took time to play with the people.

Chapter 9

QUICK-FIX MISSIONS

SHORT-TERM MISSIONS is the wave of the future. There is a mind set that says we can get anything we need these days, including a heart for missions, in short digestible doses. However, the quick-fix approach to missions seems to short-circuit career commitment. Parachuting people in for concentrated cross-cultural exposure, and airlifting them out with a minimum of discomfort, appears to do disservice to the Great Commission call to "GO". Career missionaries are automatically suspicious of short cut approaches to anything.

So what do you do, when you want to do something? As a career missionary, I, for one, am a thorough believer in the short-term system, not as an alternative to the career model, but as a motivator for career commitment to global missions. It is important, however, to evaluate why you want to go on a short-term assignment.

The Parachute Approach

I wonder if some people opt for a short-term experience just to soothe their Great Commission conscience, with what I call a parachute approach to cross-cultural exposure. The choice of terminology is deliberate. A few years ago a letter came to our field executive committee from an individual requesting permission to visit our field with a most unique ministry in mind.

The man was an ex-paratrooper who had fallen in love with Jesus and wanted to put his jumping skill to work for the Lord. He was asking for permission to fly over the Amazon jungle and parachute Bibles into the

Indian tribes of the region. His sincerity could not be doubted. His sanity perhaps.

Besides the fact that he appeared to want to bypass the lifetime of translation work it would take to get the Bible into the language of some of those tribes, this “Jump For Jesus” mission, as we dubbed it, would have to be scrubbed for other reasons. Drug patrol planes in the area would not have stopped to interview the man dropping into the jungle with a big package under his arm before they dropped him, and his plane, out of the sky. Managing to evade military patrols would have been a merciful beginning to a miserable end at the hands of tribes who see the North American as the great invader, and whose thirst for oil has been shrinking their hunting ground and ruining their culture. Wisely and kindly, we thanked the man for his offer, and declined.

There are short-term project organizers whose plans for instant missions, though not quite as adventuresome, can be just as ambitious. The parachute approach is still alive today. If you read a natural skepticism into the response to your offer to assist a missionary friend with his work, it may well be that he has had a less than positive experience with would-be parachutists.

A genuine desire to help the resident missionary with his work is widespread in the churches I visit in North America. Enthusiasm for short-term assignments is almost epidemic. We want to do something, we really want to help, I hear them saying. The bottom line is that the career missionary is not sure there's anything for short termers to do, and less than sure that they can do it.

PRACTICAL POINTERS

Here are some practical ways you can make a short-term experience of long-term impact.

1. Be humble about what you have to offer.

For me the key to a successful short-term work team is low profile, high performance. It's hard to maintain a low profile in a low roofed bus. Just ask my colleague Joel. As a keen first termer he was anxious to impress with his coolness on a trip to a jungle church. We piled onto the bus with all the grace of a couple of lumberjacks, back packs in hand. Stepping over the sacks of produce strewn in the aisle, we threw ourselves as inconspicuously as possible toward our assigned seats. It has always amazed me how the locals can maneuver themselves through the logjam without a ruffle. When we had shoehorned ourselves into the narrow seats, I noticed that blood was trickling from Joel's forehead. He had smashed his head on the overhead hand rail and was patting away the blood. Not wanting to draw attention to himself, he had bitten his tongue and pushed on. The point is that as foreigners, unfamiliar with all the intricacies of this other world, we try not to draw attention to ourselves, but usually fail.

A loud rah-rah approach to a work team project is not the approach we are looking for. The well-honed foreman-directed crew may not work where you are going. Be flexible. Remember, you are aiming at short-term contact that will produce a long-term impact.

> *"Let us not become weary in doing good, for at the proper time we will reap a harvest if we do not give up. Therefore, as we have opportunity, let us do good to all people, especially to those who belong to the family of believers."*
>
> Galatians 6:9,10

Your missions encounter is one of those opportunities to "do good." In fact, you may be confronted with more opportunities to "do good" than you will know how to handle. Here are some things I have found helpful in sorting out how much "good" I should be doing, and when and where.

A. Doing good is hard work.

Doing good is more than simply responding to a good feeling I have toward someone. Some projects are just plain hard work. It is often easier to toss money at a beggar on the street from the window of my car than to take him to a bakery to buy him bread. Doing good always takes effort so don't give up.

B. Doing good can be misunderstood.

Not everything we do for others will be well received. Some may be suspicious of our motives or think we are flaunting our wealth. What you accomplish through your work trip may not be appreciated till long after you leave. Doing good has an element of faith to it. Let's be modest about how we express our good works so we don't communicate that we have come to show them HOW. It is always better to do things with people, than for them. *How* we do good is just as important as *what* we do.

C. Doing good has a spiritual dimension.

You will not be able to help everyone who asks. Don't try. The Bible is clear: "*ESPECIALLY to those who belong to the family of believers.*" Most projects are designed to DO GOOD to some of the family of believers. Handing out relief to an individual who does not understand the spiritual dimension of our act often creates more of a victim who will be looking for another handout down the road. There are, of course, desperate cases that demand our compassion. Christian people with genuine needs, however, have the spiritual capacity to receive "good deeds" as a spiritual act. God gives them the grace to be gracious receivers. Though it may be more blessed to give than to receive, it takes more grace to receive than to give. Don't just dump things on people. Give with grace! Allow people the opportunity to receive help with dignity because we have given in humility.

2. Be good at what you came to do.

This plea comes from personal experience. Somehow, somewhere, the idea has sifted into the developed world that anything we can do for a developing country will be better than what they have. That is only a half-truth. We get letters! Some of them sound all too much like the one below.

Dear Missionary BOB,

We are arriving June 1 and would like to know if there is any way we can be of use to you on the field. We have read your recent prayer letter and are willing
to do anything you may have for us such as paint the radio tower, put the roof on the jungle church, or rewire your Indian school. Our group of 55 is made up of 49 ladies from our Golden Glow sunset group, a Christian ballerina, a computer chip inspector, an angioplasty technician, and a dinosaur scientist who would like to know how to join up with any expeditions in the area. He is able to show an excellent creationist film on the subject, in the evenings, to the natives. You would have to translate the film for him because it is only in English
We have arranged to bring prepackaged dietetic milk shake meal units for most of our group so we won't be a bother to you for breakfast. All they require is filtered chlorine-free water to mix up. The other meals will need to be served on a strict six-hour rotation, but as long as they are low cal, fat free, decaf and fiber-enriched we will eat anything.
Twelve of our team are part of a Christian discipleship weight loss pact and will need 45 minutes each morning to do their aerobics. As you can see, we are a very normal, average bunch of people and would like to have the chance to sing a chorus we learned from a missionary on tour last year. We don't know if he was from your country or not but we think they would like the music. Be assured that we do not want to inconvenience you in any way and want to be flexible and helpful.
PS One of our ladies would like to do puppet mime.

DISCLAIMER: Any similarity between this letter and one you may have recently written is purely coincidental.

While the exaggeration is for effect, I'm sure you get the point. The problems created by a visiting work team are not unsimilar. Special diets or schedules, lone ranger dinosaur scientists or anyone else with a private agenda, people with plenty of willingness but lacking the skills to do the jobs needed, or people who want to have a public ministry but have no defined ministry or language skills can all rattle the host missionary's cage, not to mention insulting the host believers.

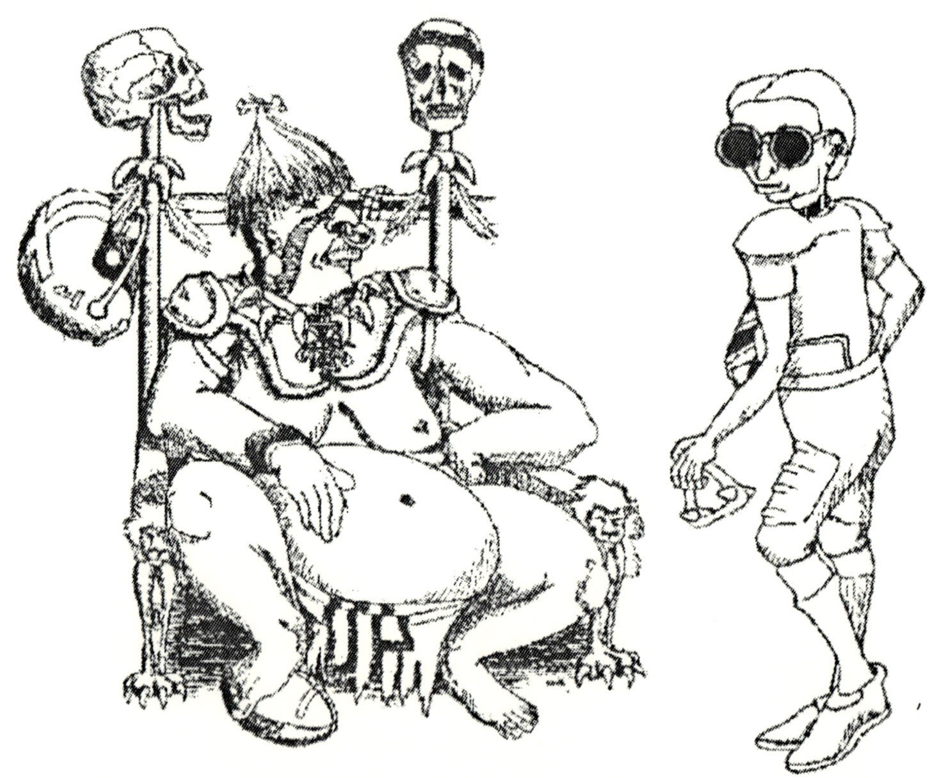

"But blocking's not my gift! Back home I usually carry the ball."

I have unfortunately seen local Christians too embarrassed to smile, but too amused not to smirk at the low grade amateur hour music that is passed off in the name of Christian ministry by people who have always dreamed of coming to the mission field to do what no home pastor would ever permit on his platform.

3. Be ready to scrub your plans on arrival.

People who come with a predetermined agenda are destined for disappointment. A work team of four came to put up a church in the jungle. The specialized equipment they brought and the energy level with which they arrived suggested they had covered every contingency and expected to raise the building single-handedly. I can understand. They had paid a good sum of money and come a long way.

They had only ten days to get the job done. What they had not counted on was mixing cement by hand, delays getting gravel, the shortage of boards to put up forms, the heat, the stomach problems, or the rain. To their credit and to the good of the local church they adapted to local methods and worked till they dropped, leaving behind, by their example of servanthood and persistence, a delicious taste in everyone's mouth, and some hefty beams that would one day be a church.

Being ready to scrub your plans may mean being ready to scrub floors. That servant spirit will go much further than any physical monument you erect. When your joyful attitude and work ethic reinforce the Scriptural principles the missionary and national pastors have been teaching, you are being most helpful to them.

4. Be modest in your expectations of public ministry.

"One of our group is bringing a violin" does not always sound like music in a host missionary's ears. While professionalism is not required or even desired, quality is appreciated. I have winced through too many attempts to impress the "natives" with a mediocre rendition of a common chorus, in a feeble imitation of their language, to be optimistic. If there are musicians in the group, they can and should be used. Learning to sing in public in a second language should only be done with plenty of practice and a good tutor to make sure the pronunciation is acceptable.

A guest singing group offered to teach a new chorus to our church, one we had already been singing for two generations. A special soloist sang for us the "Via de la Rosa" (it translates "the way of the rose"), instead of the "*Via Dolorosa*" (literally a reference to the "path of pain" Christ walked on his way to the cross).

An African missionary watched in horror as an enthusiastic short-termer joined in a worship dance reserved for the elderly women of the church. Besides making a mockery of their ministry he created a large credibility problem for the missionary that took months to repair, long after the short-termer had triumphantly reported to his home church on his adaptability at "worshipping with them."

Combining ministry with a physical work experience is also tricky. The language barrier is formidable. Mime works. And programs like *Church*

Partner Evangelism are attempting to fill the gap. Evangelism teams join hands with local church people to make evangelistic contacts. Through bilingual printed materials the visitor does very little speaking but supports the national by his presence and his prayers. The program has seen significant numbers of conversions, has stimulated personal evangelism in the local churches, and is administered so that missionaries do not get caught in the middle doing taxiing and translating.

5. Be balanced in your perception of real needs.

There is a special fascination with the poor. As if it were somehow more spiritual, the average tour group gravitates naturally and emotionally to the poor end of the social spectrum. Missionary hosts of tour groups are quite capable of manipulating the sentiments and pocket books of visiting tour teams simply by choosing what to show them.

Following a long, hot tour through the various sectors of the urban sprawl of Guayaquil, pointing out major and important church planting projects going on in middle and upper class areas, I chose to drive the group up to Mapasingue, a bamboo shack town that had been built overnight ten years before by masses of poor that had invaded an entire hill. The group was impressed. The earlier lessons of the morning were totally lost by the impact this lower class district made on them. I was not really surprised when a special offering arrived a few months later from the sending church wanting to help the Mapasingue congregation with their church building. I did not begrudge the gift, but the Mapasingue experience taught me to be cautious in what I show people. The other projects among middle and upper class proportionally required much more faith and resources than the simple sanctuary going up in Mapasingue, but they did not capture the imagination of the visitors. What they do not know is that I could have taken them to a district that for pure shock value would have left Mapasingue well in the dust.

A visiting delegation from Canada was looking over potential projects as part of a partner church plan established by our denomination. The tour guide decided to drive them past a small Indian church starting up in the city. To our surprise the delegation decided that the Indian church, not an approved project by either mission or national church standards, was what they wanted to support. To their great credit, that church accepted the advice of mission leaders and is actively participating with the approved partner church congregation. Yet I'm sure that for some of them at least, their hearts are still with the Indian church on the outskirts of town.

Trusting what a missionary says in terms of real need is not always easy. The other needs look so desperate. The missionary who shows you a shack town suburb may seem singularly unmoved by the heart-wrenching emotions you are just now feeling. Understanding the career missionary is essential to being sensitive in this area. The average missionary is a profile in plodding. Most of them are in it for the long haul. They have probably been to the shack town a dozen times. They may have an inside track on life in the poor neighborhoods. For instance, some marginal communities have hired strong-men lawyers to support their rights to the invasion of municipal land or private property. These invasion groups throw up any kind of a shack on a lot just to lay possession to it. Such instant slums produce grave problems for urban two-thirds world governments who feel pressured to provide basic services to these aggressive groups at the expense of other tax-paying citizens who are more pacific in their demeanor. Indian groups, which seem so poor in the city, may actually have an agricultural community base back in the country to support their church expansion that other resident groups in the city could never hope to have.

ORIENTATION CHECKLIST:

How to plan for a project

- ❑ Motivate the church by building a missions prayer cell.
- ❑ Obtain denominational approval.
- ❑ Contact the field well in advance. There is a need to coordinate guest house facilities and missionary teaching schedules, furlough dates, field conferences, and family vacations.
- ❑ Establish a selection process with teeth in it. Being a nice guy and letting everyone go who wants to takes some of the heat off you, but dilutes the importance of the experience.
- ❑ Enlist the entire church in some way or other. Involve people to help with purchasing, to prepare devotional materials, or to support someone who wants to go but can't afford it. This will insure that there will be an ongoing prayer base.
- ❑ Outline your orientation schedule. Ask the missionary for advice here. He may have material to share, such as a video. Include practical sessions in language tutoring with experts.
- ❑ Maintain communication with your host missionary to keep him motivated. He will keep it on the back burner as long as he can. Without being demanding, push for specifics on the projects to be done. Ask what will be your financial responsibility toward the projects. Are there materials or tools you need to bring? Send a

list of the people in the group, their ages, skills, and special interests. Include any special needs of the group in terms of diet, rest or travel.

PLANNING FOR CLOSURE

- ❑ Closure is important. Allow time in your schedule for the last-minute farewells and goodbye parties people may want to shower on you.
- ❑ Plan to leave "*recuerdos.*" It means "souvenirs by which to remember our relationship"(like lapel pins of your flag, for instance). Special relationships could be recognized with more personal items. Depending on the social level, a T-shirt, hat, or pair of shoes, if appropriate, can be an appreciated token of your friendship. Consult your host before doing things that will set unreasonable precedents like leaving your camera with someone. That could create more hard feelings than happy memories. One of our work teams had fun dividing up all the good tools they brought among the men on the project, but even with my help bad feelings were not avoided.
- ❑ It is better to promise nothing than to be generous in offering to write, send pictures you have taken, or come back next year, but by God's grace do more than you promised. SEND back a picture of yourself and the national hosts working together. WRITE a letter of appreciation. I had to face a little ten year old girl every time I went back to visit a jungle church where short-termers had visited, trying to give new excuses for why they had not written as they promised.
- ❑ If a second trip is possible, it is always better to try to concentrate on a longer term relationship with a particular local church or country than to do a lot of globetrotting.

Chapter 10

GOING ANYWAY

W*HO DID YOU SAY was going to Guyana this summer?* Short-term ministry is not a short-cut to ministry. Some form of selection must be built into the orientation process. If you are planning to launch a short-term missions experience in the near future, this is for you.

Called but Not Cut Out

In a chapter entitled "The Myth of the Call," Sunder Krishnan dispels the notion of a mystical revelation that is required before one can be sure he has been chosen by God to do the dirty work of missions. For Krishnan, a converted Hindu, the Great Commission is for everyone. "If you conclude you're not called to serve cross culturally, then you are automatically part of the group called to serve by living counter culturally."[3]

Not everyone is cut out for cross cultural ministry. But there is nothing like a short-term assignment to find out. For that reason there is validity in getting as many people as possible exposed to a second culture. Consider yourself called. The only question to settle is whether you are cut out for it or not.

This chapter is aimed at people who are in the final stages of deciding on some form of cross-cultural service. There is an important spiritual principle that needs to be addressed. The Lord always selects and sifts the men and women he chooses to send. The lesson can be learned from the life of judge Gideon. Judges 7:1-7 narrates an unusual sequence of

---

[3] Krishnan. p. 69.

tests in his final selection process. Today we would call it jumping through the right hoops.

The judge's selection procedure teaches us that people do not fail to qualify for ministry as often as they disqualify themselves from it. When Gideon was looking for recruits he placed a general muster call in the press. But not everybody got to go with Gideon. Nor did everyone want to. There was a system of selection, and if your service for the Lord is to be honored and blessed, there should be some hoops for you, and your people, to jump through, too.

Warm Bodies, or Fresh Blood

God is not desperate for recruits. The laborers may be "few" but there are still laborers available. God will not take anyone He can get. Mission agencies may, and local churches sometimes do, but the Lord of the Harvest is still hand-picking his personnel. It was a President of the Central American Mission who wrote that his mission was not looking for warm bodies, but for fresh blood. And so is the Lord.

With Gideon's enemies swarming like flies in the valley below, it did not seem like a time for the recruiting agency to be getting picky. It was ludicrous that the Lord should call for a culling of the candidates with such an enormous task at hand.

Some would suggest that with 70% of the world's non-Christians unable to hear the gospel unless someone leaves his or her culture to enter a second culture and tell them of Christ, you'd think they wouldn't be so fussy about accreditation interviews, home service, language aptitudes and character attitudes, and all the other seemingly ridiculous requirements for career missionary service. There are those who are engaging in short-term or freelance cross-cultural exposure precisely because they can not fulfill the lengthy commitment required to be a full time cross-cultural minister.

If career service calls for selective recruiting, I'm convinced that every short-term assignment or work team ministry should incorporate some aspect of selection. God always selected and sifted the men he sent. The crisis before Gideon was a time for mustering every able-bodied man available, but right in the middle of the most excruciating candidate crisis imaginable, the Lord told Gideon to trim the roster. "Not just warm bodies, Gideon. I want fresh blood."

The Lord was obviously looking for men with a lust to fight, not just people who decided to show up because they had nothing better to do that summer. As uncomfortable as the realities of cross-cultural ministry may present themselves to you, some of you have decided that you must go whatever it takes. You are scared, but you are going anyway! As uncomfortable as the prospect of a piece of the action may appear, the alternative is unthinkable.

Seven young men and myself were preparing to trek into a remote region of Ecuador that had never been reached by evangelical missionaries. It stands out in my mind as the trip I almost didn't make. As we were planning to go, the most incredible combination of discouraging circumstances and demoralizing obstacles converged on the calendar to make us want to cancel out. When I suggested to Hope that perhaps we'd better not go, she offered one of those golden gems of wifely wisdom that we hate to hear: "You know you'll be more miserable if you don't go than if you do."

She was right! I lost twelve pounds and went lame on the trail. Miserable it was. There were no mules. There was mud on the mountain up to our knees. But was I glad I had gone!

Seven people made decisions to make Christ Lord of their lives. A church was born. Later visits led to more fruit. The story of the adventure became an article, and then the chapter of a book that has inspired many. And all because I went, if only grudgingly. God is looking for people who are going anyway, even though they might prefer to do other things. And here is how he found them.

There are two distinct ways the Lord weeded out Gideon's workers. In two dramatic cuts Gideon reduced his roster to 1% of the original volunteers. In the first single sweeping reduction he wiped out a full 2/3 of the fighting force. Then the Lord told Gideon that the army was still too large, not in terms of the size of the enemy, but "too many for me."(Judges 7:2) In the second cut, only 300 of the final 10,000 made the grade. Gideon's graduating class was disappointingly small.

One of the pet peeves of missionaries hosting short-term personnel is that local churches insist on sending everyone who can afford a ticket. My personal limit for a manageable team is twelve. There is something healthy and spiritual about a selection process.

In both of the methods Gideon employed to trim down the troops, we see mirrored the manner in which men and women rule themselves out of the ministry today. The methodology is not sophisticated. Gideon employed two tactics: A questionnaire and a spot-check quiz.

The Question

The questionnaire was simple: a single "yes" or "no" question. Do you want to go? It was an application form with a single blank. Willingness to go may not be the only criteria for cross-cultural ministry, but it's a vital first step. The first group of candidates was disqualified by the process of self-elimination. They didn't really want to go. Not everyone got to go because not everyone wanted to go. They were disqualified by personal fear.

A college in which I taught trains young people for Christian ministry. Fifty percent of the freshman class did not return for a second year. You would think that people enrolling in an institution whose expressed purpose was to train people for ministry would have an inkling of interest in ministry. Yet half of them dropped out after a year. If you have a sense that God wants you in cross-cultural service of some sort, stick with the troops. God never begs for recruits. Twenty-two thousand of Gideon's freshman candidates said they had seen enough when asked a single simple question. "Do you want to stay home?" Don't be one of them. You'll be more miserable than if you go!

Leaders of short-term ministry programs must exercise an element of recruiting toughness. A youth team leader scheduled a boot camp work experience as part of his orientation program. Some of the group decided to skip the event, but somehow got on the plane with the group when the good stuff was about to happen. Some people, by missing out on the training phase, are just saying, "I don't really want to go!"

What are your fears? Deal with them and go anyway! Some people apply for ministry and are surprised when they are actually chosen. I recall the half-buried wish I had that my mission leaders would find some gaping hole in my profile and refuse to take me. I was almost disappointed when I was appointed. They can't have done all the tests. If they only knew the real me, they wouldn't have accepted me.

A pastor's wife was being administered a harsh tongue lashing by a member of the church for her shortcomings and sins. When the church member was finished, the pastor's wife asked if that were all. Then she silenced her critic by adding these words, "My dear sister, if you knew what I was really like inside, you wouldn't even be standing here talking to me." Adequacy for ministry does not depend on our ability as much as on our availability.

Paul, the prototype missionary, said: "*I am well content with weaknesses, with insults, with distresses, with persecutions, with difficulties for Christ's sake; for when I am weak, then am I strong.*" (2 Corinthians 12:9,10) If there are nagging fears, insecurities, feelings of inferiority or inadequacy, the Lord says "*My grace is sufficient for you, for my power is perfected in weakness.*" You do not need to let personal fear disqualify you from ministry as it did for 22,000 in Gideon's day.

Gideon himself was a Class A coward, who hid in the wine press from the enemy, and who didn't dare to face his father's household in the daylight. He did his dirty work after dark. In Judges 7, the Lord told him that the work team was down to size and that it was time to go, BUT if

Gideon was afraid, he could sneak up to the camp by himself and snoop on the Midianites. And the mighty warrior leader actually did it! The fact that he went on this private night scouting trip was a clear admission that personal fear was always a problem for Gideon. But it was not a fear that crippled him or prevented him from doing what needed to be done.

What are your fears? "*I sought the Lord,*" said the valiant giant slayer David, "*and he heard me and delivered me from all my fears.*" (Psalm 34:4) Some people miss out on ministry because they are afraid that God can't use them, while some are just afraid that he might. Watchman Nee said that "Lowliness is not looking down on one's self; rather it is not looking at one's self at all." He goes on to say, "Timidity is not humility. While humility is self forgetfulness completely—a forgetting both of its weakness and strength—timidity recalls all the weakness and hence is self-remembering." In the end, successful ministry for you, your family, or your work team, will not be in learning whether you have what it takes, but in learning to let Him take what you have. The experience ahead for you may not be as much a time of discovering your strengths, as it is a time of exposing your weaknesses.

The Quiz

The second hoop Gideon asked his men to jump through was a surprise spot-check. His spontaneous quiz caught more than a few men completely off guard. It teaches a second principle in the sifting and selection process. Not everyone got to go, simply because he wanted to go. Some people eliminated themselves... by personal failure.

"That's not fair," I hear you say. "They never told us they were watching." The General's pop quiz caught them napping. This group of candidates eliminated themselves through a foolish lapse. I'm sure there were those who grumbled, "We never knew it would be on the exam. How were we supposed to know how Gideon expected us to drink water?" It was, at worst, a careless slip, but the spot-check at the brook caught 10,000 men off guard.

How many people eliminate themselves from significant service by some momentary minor lapse? The short-term cross-cultural experience you are considering may be your personal brook experience, but remember that the battle begins at the brook.

I can hear the locker room bad mouthing as Gideon asks 10,000 men to turn in their uniforms. "It was just a practice witness weekend." "It's only orientation." "This is only language study." But the spot-check at the brook was more than some gimmick for getting the army down to manageable size. It was more than a dry run dress rehearsal. Resist the mentality that your short-term assignment or work team project is only for six weeks, or only for a year or two. What you do at the brook will reveal how you can expect to do in the battle.

When I went to Ecuador as a summer Youth Corps volunteer, I was billeted with a young seminary student. Twelve years later, when I returned to Ecuador, that seminary student was now a member of the Board of Directors of the National Church, and a pivotal person in the delicate dealings between the mission and the National Church. A short-term cross-cultural ministry opportunity may seem like a casual drink at the brook, but it could return to haunt you, or help you, in years to come. Don't forget that the battle begins at the brook.

Never let down your guard. Gideon's men admitted they were not afraid to fight, but they disqualified themselves by a foolish lapse. If there is some small area of personal weakness you have not given over to the Lordship of Christ, it is not too minor to mess up your ministry. Things so insignificant as drink or dress, reading or recreation, music or manners can cut you off from serious consideration as a soldier of Jesus Christ and drastically curtail your effectiveness. I am not talking about legalistic living. I am simply saying that "*No man who serves as a soldier gets involved in civilian affairs . . . he wants to please his commanding officer.*" (2 Timothy 2:4)

Another example is so minor I hate to mention it, but it had such an effect that I can't afford not to. A Youth Corps visitor to our home in Loja sat down to breakfast with our family and served himself a big bowl of Raisin Bran for breakfast. Sounds innocent enough, doesn't it? What the young man hadn't picked up was what we had said about the value of a box of Raisin Bran in those parts. Raisin Bran from Grand Rapids, Michigan, came into Ecuador at considerable expense, and arrived in Loja at even greater expense and effort. It was a luxury item to which we treated ourselves once a week. The box we set out for our guests was to last the entire summer until the children returned to school. It was a special summer treat we had decided to share with our guests.

But then the enthusiastic guest proceeded to serve himself a second heaping bowl. "We love Raisin Bran at Hudson College," he said. "It's all we need to eat for breakfast."

The kids glanced from the bowl back to mom to see what she would say. We gulped and said nothing as we watched him wolfing down our imported Raisin Bran.

The incident was over, as far as I was concerned, until I found a thank you note from this same fellow on my desk, outlining some of the things he felt needed work in my home, including my marriage. Had he not already left, I would have probably been tempted to choke him to death with what was left of the Raisin Bran.

I said it was a silly thing. Just a bowl of Raisin Bran. But by a small slip-up he had effectively cut himself off from any possible ministry to us. If he was unable to read the significance of a box of Raisin Bran to a missionary family, how could he be trusted to read the spiritual tone of that same missionary family? Gideon, too, turned back 10,000 men who were just a little over anxious at the trough.

Don't blow it over a bowl of Raisin Bran, or an extra five minutes of hot water in the shower that the host has rationed to three minutes. My mentor, Dr. Arnold Cook, used to tell us on the Canadian Bible College hockey team, " A gentleman is known by his conduct at the table and in the game . . . and so is a Christian!" Some people suggest by their style of play that "what we do across that painted line may be ministry, but THIS IS HOCKEY!" Some of our greatest ministry opportunities may be missed by "messing up" in some of life's most basic areas, and something as ridiculous as a second bowl of Raisin Bran may rule you out of really meaningful ministry. People do not, as a rule, fail to qualify for ministry as often as they disqualify themselves from it.

I'm convinced that there were men who wanted to be a part of Gideon's small band of warriors, but who could not get a handle on their personal fears. I am equally convinced that many well-qualified men were left standing at the brook, disqualified by a momentary personal failure, an indiscretion, a slight indifference, or perhaps just indecision. A temporary relaxation of the rules cut them off from being part of something they had been ready to die for.

The most miserable day of a short-term missions trip I took was when I took time off to go to the beach with some North American tourists. The beach party was innocent enough, but a momentary slip when the missionary and my fellow team members were not around cut me off from ministry to the tourists. It is always a part of my inner record, because I decided to relax the rules just a little when the right people weren't looking!

Don't disqualify yourself from opportunities just around the corner. God is not in the business of begging for volunteers. He is not looking for a few more warm bodies to fill out his depleted roster. He wants fresh blood... people ready and willing to do what it costs to count for Him. He wants men and women who understand that the battle begins at the brook. God is looking for people so desperate to serve Him cross-culturally that no personal fear can keep them back. And he is looking for people so committed to serve Him that they will not allow a moment of weakness to rob them of that desire.

In the end, it will not be a question of whether you have what it takes, but whether you will let him take what you have, your willingness along with your weakness. Remember it is His name that is at stake, not yours! It is His Kingdom you are promoting, not some personal proving ground. It is His reputation that is being risked, not yours, as much as you may feel threatened, embarrassed, intimidated or observed. *"It is the Lord Christ you serve."*

A scared-stiff rookie seaman looking at the ominous waves over the North Sea questioned his captain's wisdom in heading out at night to help a vessel in trouble. "We'll never get back," he protested.

The veteran British rescue tug captain only tightened his grip on the helm. "We don't have to come back, sailor. But we *do* have to go."

AN ORIENTATION EXERCISE:

The Right Stuff

- ❑ Design your own selection process whether a boot camp or a local community service activity. Make participation obligatory, and stick with the rules, even if the pastor's kid gets cut. Why not require reading this book as part of the selection process. Call for the completion of assignments such as writing out responses to these critical questions.
- ❑ Stage a mock "baggage party" where you talk about what you will take, and what you should not take. Use it as an opportunity to challenge your group to travel light and not to assume that just because it is a short trip, and a long way from home, there are some liberties you will allow yourself.

1. What are the things in my life that could keep trip me up on this trip if they ever got loose? Use a suitcase in this orientation session and have everyone write on a slip of paper some item they might not want their team leader to know they were bringing. Stuff it in the suitcase, then ask the group how to dispose of the "stuff" before they travel. The range of doubtful baggage people bring on short-term trips can be anything from a pornographic Internet habit to an indiscriminate appetite for Raisin Bran.
2. What are my biggest fears about going with the group? Discuss and pray about them together. Then honestly ask yourself, Do I want to go, regardless? If the answer is "yes", start packing your suitcase. With the right stuff.

Chapter 11

LEAVING EARLY

ONE OF THE NATURAL PHENOMENON of transition is the tendency to leave early. A college president reminded a faculty meeting that some of the strange behavior we were witnessing on campus six weeks before Christmas was due to the fact that some of the students had already left. No, they had not finished their course work, checked in their cafeteria cards, or turned in their room keys. They were still present physically, but had left emotionally. For all intents and purposes they were no longer with us. While the reentry phenomenon will be more complex, the longer one has been away, many of these same emotions come into play when coming back from a short-term cross cultural encounter.

People may "leave early" from experiences that have been draining, or where they have sensed failure or in acceptance, or they may "leave early" because of the heightened anticipation of going home. Missionaries leave early, as well. They are still winding down engagements and completing responsibilities, but emotionally they have already left. It seems that some missionaries have geared their whole metabolism to that magic moment when it is time to go home. Like a regressive countdown, an unconscious clock is ticking away inside them, marking the months and minutes until liftoff.

Unfortunately the passion to "get out of here" betrays the assurances to one and all that we really do "like it here" and can't wait to get back. The missionary who has been anticipating his home assignment for several months may forget that national friends are not as eager for the date to arrive.

Short-term workers, especially, can underestimate the importance of "closure." They have done their thing, had contact with another culture, met some great national Christians, and are now ready to get back home and on with their lives. The national Christians, on the other hand, who have opened themselves, and often their homes, to these fly-in visitors, now feel torn by the sad fact that the short-termer confesses he has no immediate plans to return. We owe it to our new national friends to realize how deeply we may have worked our way into their lives, and not to leave without properly disengaging.

The urge to get back home does not hit everyone the same way. Short-term missions personnel will not experience the phenomenon to the same degree. Yet that urge to get back to the Snickers bars after two weeks of famine relief in Mali may be just as strong. Don't cheat on your "check-out" time. In the words of my missionary mentor Arnold Cook, "Wherever you are be all there." Determine to be "all there" till the wheels fold up in the belly of the plane.

To adequately understand and adapt to the itch for the familiar wrappers of our lives, as well as to be able to minister to the unique needs of the person undergoing a transcultural transition, it is important to say something about the transition back. The cultural comfort zone of the average North American is often as close or as far away as the nearest Snickers chocolate bar.

The visiting father of a missionary colleague became so depressed on a short visit to the field that he invaded a local store specializing in North American goods, stormed to the counter and demanded, "Give me chocolate bars." Price was no object. What he ached for was the assurance of something familiar. I have seen on the faces of visiting work teams the same homesick yearning for a particular chain restaurant or a popular franchise hardware store.

My children grew to associate "home" with Snickers bars, something they never thought of buying when they were at home in Canada. They were just more comfortable with a Snickers bar buried deep in their bedroom. Near the end of a term my wife would discover the moldy remains of half-eaten North American candy at the bottom of more than one dresser drawer. It was not the chocolate they craved. Like the man in the store, they were more in love with the wrapper.

The first-term missionary is usually hardest hit by the urge to find out if all the good things he left are still back there waiting for him. As the moment approaches, anticipation intensifies. When furlough fever finally hits, it can produce cravings as irrational as anything a pregnancy has ever concocted. Visions of Big Macs and Snickers bars invade their dreams. Family vacations, evenings together, outings and sports events, hobbies, enrichment courses, television favorites and a whole host of unrealized childhood ambitions creep into the cranium and crowd out mission work. Elaborate grocery lists of things to be done on furlough flood the mind. Like a sailor on shore-leave the missionary can face furlough as a year-long fix of his favorite things.

Being aware of the normal tensions of the returning missionary can help to ease anyone back into his home culture. Consider some common experiences he will encounter on his passage back into what he thought was an old familiar world.

Cultural Conversion

The experience of returning to a home culture is similar to a conversion experience. It's like being born-again culturally the first time you face it. Getting reacquainted with once reflex activities can be disquieting. I remember our family's first stop at a corner convenience store after getting off the plane. I almost expected someone to yell at me when I reached for a chocolate bar to carry it to the till. We had spent a term in a rural setting where every piece of store merchandise was bolted down or behind the counter and had to be asked for. Not touching something until it was paid for had become more a part of me than I realized.

Our children's favorite stop at Disney World, fresh out of Latin America, was the drinking fountain. After four years of being yelled at, *"Don't drink the water,"* a public dispenser of drinkable water was a magic kingdom all its own.

My rear-pocket wallet had been a constant companion since grade school. Suddenly, in Costa Rica, everyone was turning in their wallets for money pouches that were looped to their belts and tucked inside the front of their pants. Off and on through the first term I recall looking wistfully at my Canadian wallet in the dresser drawer, the remaining change from my last commercial exchange in another world still inside. Coming back into Canadian culture was to experience that wallet withdrawal, in reverse.

I discovered a fascination with freeways and divided highways, smooth sidewalks and straight stretches of road and all the comforts of cruise-control living. Taking a mental, and preferably written, note of these immediate impressions of your return will help cement the significance of your time away.

The Smorgasbord Syndrome

The returnee to a home culture probably comes from a world where the supermarket had only one variety of milk, if any at all when you wanted it. She did not need to worry about whether it was fat free, 2%, skim milk, whole milk or any variety other than sour. When she sent her kid to the corner store for eggs, she exulted in seeing him swinging the plastic bag of eggs, irregardless of grade or color. It makes the first stroll through a North American supermarket a near worshipful walk. My wife cried. Another missionary confessed to walking out without buying anything. There was just too much to choose from. Sprawling salad bar spreads are a microcosm of our whole consumer society. The infinite variety of goods and services is a shock to the system.

The urge to indulge is a natural consequence of having been away. Choosing to deliberately deny himself some exquisite delight for even a few hours will help the returnee to take his first step of commitment to a cross cultural lifestyle. The practical task at the end of this chapter suggests signing a "Declaration of Solidarity with the Concept of Less".

The Treadmill Effect

Another phenomenon of returning to a home culture is what I call the treadmill effect. A treadmill may be a good aerobic experience but if you have any illusions about getting anywhere you are on the wrong machine. Friends and peers who waved you off with tears and promises of loyal support have gone on to other things. For the career missionary they are four years of mortgage payments further down the road from you. They may be a snowmobile, a recreational vehicle or a second degree removed from you.

The sense that the missionary is losing ground socially and materially is only reinforced when he goes home. He may go through the motions of fitting back into his culture but he can see the floor slipping out from under him. A missionary is someone who deliberately distances himself from his own culture in order to obey the Great Commission. Anyone who thinks he can serve the Lord as a career foreign missionary without losing ground in his own culture is only kidding himself. To be an effective change agent in another culture it will cost you, in many respects, your own.

For the short-termer there has been a distancing as well, though more subtle. Your friends cannot possibly share your deepest impressions. They have been living on a different emotional wavelength. Even in the short space of time you were away events have occurred in your lives that you have not shared with each other. On the other hand, they may not be able to understand your reaction to some of their perceived waste, or their casual indifference to some creature comfort. You've changed and they may not understand the new you.

Growing gradually uncomfortable with one's native culture is a job hazard of the career cross-cultural minister. Understanding what is happening during the reentry to a home culture may not make it any more comfortable, but understanding that it does occur can ease the pain.

For the short-term worker, the task only *seems* simpler. Most cross-cultural exposure leaves its scars, if only an uneasiness with the way things are. We are still talking about a contact sport. It may be easier to submerge yourself in the host culture with a six-week supply of Snickers bars in your briefcase, but the return home will take its inevitable toll, especially coming back to a culture whose lowest common denominator of a comfort zone is probably a candy bar.

Preparing for CLOSURE AND REENTRY

To avoid cheating on your "check-out" time, schedule a "closure" into your calendar. Some travelers are so paranoid about getting out of a place that they waste their last days or hours washing next week's clothes or plotting next week's agenda instead of "being all there" till the final buzzer. Block out time to say good-bye properly to your national or missionary hosts. Make the decision ahead of time not to "leave early" regardless how hard the experience has been.

AN ORIENTATION EXERCISE

REENTRY

Before you set out on your cross-cultural experience, make a list of the five creature comforts you will most miss. Life would be unbearable if I had to do without these five things for the rest of my life.

While you are in the host culture, and as they occur to you, make a second list of people and things you will be grateful for when you get back home.

- public services like pay telephones, public washrooms, or public transit transfers.
- parking meters and free route maps.
- automated tellers and information kiosks.
- people such as friendly checkout persons, highway patrolmen, or mail delivery personnel.
- specialized church ministry personnel.

Methodically work your way through the list when you get back home, writing thank-you notes or making phone calls to the people or institutions that provide these privileges in your church or community. Pack a stack of thank-you cards in your carry-on and do these notes before you clear customs.

Deliberately delay for 24 hours your participation in the five most exquisite experiences of your "old" world as a quiet statement to yourself that your wants must always be subservient to your needs.

- ✔ A Big Mac
- ✔ an extended hot shower
- ✔ ice cream
- ✔ a game of bowling
- ✔ my own car
- ✔ a can of cream corn
- ✔ a salad bar
- ✔ a video rental
- ✔ the mall
- ✔ a special breakfast cereal
- ✔ a Snickers bar

Chose one of the items from your hit list of five favorite sensations and fill out the following statement on the last evening in the country. Sign the declaration and make yourself accountable to someone else to keep your word.

A DECLARATION OF SOLIDARITY WITH THE CONCEPT OF LESS

I ________________________ declare that the experiences of having traveled and worked in _________________ for _______ days/months has indelibly altered my world view. I purposefully determine to delay my enjoyment of _________________ for ________________hours/days as a silent statement of my solidarity with the people of _____________ and my intention to deliberately limit myself to less.

Signed: _______________ Witnessed: ______________

"For where your treasure is, there will your heart be also."

Chapter 12

COMING TO STAY

A VISITOR TO EUROPE STEPPED OUT OF HIS HOTEL the first morning to take in the sights of sidewalk cafes and sidewalk artists intent on capturing on canvas the panorama of a well-groomed park back- dropped by a vast Gothic cathedral.

Within minutes one of the painters presented him with a freshly painted canvas of the scene, including, to the visitor's surprise, a representation of the visitor himself set in the foreground of the painting. It was too striking a likeness to pass up. He bought the piece on the spot.

Time passed and the visitor became a familiar sight to the artists and residents of the town. One day after a morning of reading in the park, he paused on his way to lunch to appreciate the product of the artists' efforts. To his chagrin, canvas after canvas was a perfect replica of the park where he had been reading, and the cathedral behind, with the empty bench where he had been sitting all morning. He did not appear in a single picture. The visitor expressed his surprise to one of the artists. "Ah, *mais oui, Monsieur*," the craftsman smiled. "Now that we are used to you, we don't see you anymore."

A time comes when the visitor to any culture merges with the landscape and is no longer seen. That undefined watershed is a moment that takes place more in the head of the stranger than in the eyes of the onlookers. He will always walk differently, look differently, talk differently, but a time comes when he no longer feels "different". He feels one with the humanity about him and at that moment he melts into the market, or bus queue, or stadium crowd, as a participator and not a spectator.

At that moment, when your comfort zone opens wide enough to embrace this new culture, you have walked through another doorway toward being a world Christian. When you start to feel that you could actually live there, you have passed the principal barrier to cross-cultural adaptation. You do not have to like everything about a culture in order to stay. You do not need to approve of everything you see in order to stay. You do not even need to look or act like the host people. But you do need to love them, and you need a grateful spirit for the place God has put you.

Living and working in another country and culture is an incredible opportunity and a decided social advantage. My eldest son, Peter, lived and studied in Ecuador for seven years. After completing a two-month training camp with an Ecuadorian professional soccer team, he compared his opportunity with that of his college teammates in North America. "I am very grateful for my upbringing," he said over breakfast one day. "None of them can do what I am doing . . . learning and playing with Latin American pros, in a foreign culture, using a foreign language."

We are not always grateful for our heritage. We sometimes feel like a prisoner in our context. Like the typical tourist, we arrive and we like it. We are surprised by what we see that is new or novel. In the blush of innocence we may even blurt out, "I think I could live here." Then some of us come back to stay, and discover that it is a different story.

It is something altogether different to unpack your suitcase... and stay. Traffic and redtape gridlocks tie us in knots, physically and emotionally. The emotion of newness fades with the first cultural collision. The initial flush of enthusiasm dims when we fall flat on our face in the language, and the "I could live here" turns all too suddenly into "Get me out of here!"

I remember our first visit to the village of *Buena Esperanza* in rural Ecuador. It is the most pastoral setting imaginable, snuggled in a fertile crevice that produces oranges, bananas, papaya, and almost anything else they care to plant. There was no real road, just a narrow two-lane mule trail. What an idyllic place, I remember thinking. The sights, the smells, were new and exciting. "I could live here," we said, at least to ourselves, at least until the dark rain clouds gathered over the mountain behind us. And then they told us that if the rain started it would not stop for four months, and the vehicle would not leave for six. Dramatically, "I could live here" turned to "I could die here," and my wife looked at me and panicked, "Get me out of here!!!"

There are, as we have said before, people who soothe their Great Commission consciences with a whisk-me-in, whisk-me-out, tour of duty in some other culture. They plan to hold their emotional breath through the whole ordeal. And then something amazing happens. While not always admitting it, something about the place or the people clicks, and they start to think of staying.

If you think you, as a short-termer, are immune to that possibility, think again. Sydney and Helga finished out their career in the Canadian civil service and came to "fill in" in our guest house for a year. Five years later they had just returned for another year. I talked with Helga when she first arrived as a cautious short-term missionary sub. She had the typical short-termer red flags up all over. "We're just here for a year," she said firmly. What she really was saying was, "Don't think you'll ever get me to stay here any longer." Five years later, her gracious spirit complemented a very functional grasp of the language and she looked and acted at home here.

Larry and Leslie went on a short-term mission to the Philippines. One day the squalor of their work situation was so bad it made Larry physically sick. Even before that he had started packing for home, early. But there in the middle of his own vomiting, God gave him such a deep injection of love for the poor people around him that Larry said, in effect, "I could live here, I could die here."

It was the seed of a missionary vision that never died. Though it took them ten years to find a way, Larry and Leslie came to serve missionary children in our mission school in Ecuador. What was noteworthy about their ministry is that they operated under a clear sense of cross cultural call. While their principal ministry was to the students of the academy, they were constantly seeking ways to walk into the host culture where they lived, to know the people, to love them, and to lead them to Christ. Without the benefit of concentrated language study granted to career field missionaries, they were at a distinct disadvantage. But, like Sydney and Helga, their short-term encounter with a wider world had turned into a long-term commitment to another culture. They are just another example of countless short-termers who "came to stay".

Anyone who dares to dabble in this business of cross-cultural ministry, regardless of how temporary the assignment, is opening himself to the distinct possibility that he may end up coming to stay. And those who have taken the plunge will likely tell you that such a fate is not the end of the world. For most of us it has been the beginning of a bright new broader world.

Wherever You Are, Be All There

So how can I begin to feel at home in a strange new place? Take time to unpack. Give yourself to the place God has put you. As Jeremiah advised the Israeli captives who had been exiled to Babylon for seventy years. *"Settle down . . . seek the peace and prosperity of the city to which I have carried you into exile. Pray to the Lord for it, because if it prospers, you too will prosper."*(Jer. 29:7) "WHEREVER YOU ARE, BE ALL THERE."

This advice applies as much to shorter-term workers as it does to veteran missionaries. Learning more about the place where you are always helps you feel more comfortable there. As I studied the history of the country where God placed me, I began to develop a deeper loyalty and respect for its culture and people. Feeling good or bad about a place has nothing to do with the place itself, and certainly not with the people who live there. It is merely the space that God has assigned you to work out his designs for your life.

"All right, Henry. Now you've gone too far! Fitting in with the culture is one thing, but this thing is smearing my make-up."

Wherever You Go, There You Are

David Pollock, who deals with cultural entry and reentry transitions, has said that the most disappointing thing about coming to a new place is discovering that "wherever you go, there you are." That may get us closer to the secret of being at home in any place than anything I know.

I tell a story on myself to remind me that people who cross cultural boundaries rarely check their egos at the border. I am a male missionary with a normal-sized male ego—Grade A large, my wife would probably add. It was a typical day on the mission field. Class 3! Everything was going wrong!

The house was a mess and the living room was full of company. Kids and luggage were everywhere. A missionary family in transition is not a pretty sight. A missionary family in transit, camping in the living room of another missionary family packing for furlough, is downright ugly. We were the family putting the finishing touches on packing, while colleagues fresh back on the field were camping in our living room.

When I got around to helping with breakfast, we discovered that we were out of milk. I naturally made a scene. It is not nice to be without milk when company is coming down the stairs for breakfast. Without a word to my wife, I dashed out to get a quart of milk.

In a matter of minutes I had the whole thing back under control . . . or so I thought! Bursting back into the house, I proudly plunked the face-saving milk on the kitchen counter. To do so I had dashed right past the table full of happy guests crunching their corn flakes with powdered milk, and not the wiser for the domestic crisis, at least not yet!

Hope was still in the kitchen when I came in with the milk. I could tell right away she was not impressed. In fact, she was mildly upset. Give us males credit for something. We can usually tell! I recall vividly that she was doing something with a very large kitchen knife. And I could also tell that an ugly scene was about to get downright messy. I had gone off half-cocked without consulting her. She looked up from what she was doing as only she can, and let it fly. "You're going to have to make up your mind what it will be: your ego or your marriage."

That's quite a choice, even for a missionary. She could just as well have used the knife. "Your ego or your wife!" It was bad enough she had said it. But she had said it almost loud enough for the guests to hear. And because my normal healthy male ego had now swollen to massive and unmanageable proportions, I was having trouble making up my mind which it would be. "Your ego or your marriage!" If only she hadn't said it so loud.

It was only with time and reflection that the swelling subsided and I was able to make an intelligent choice. I am still married. However, my healthy male ego still threatens, on occasion, to lay some uncomfortable options in my path. More often than I care to be reminded, I am faced with the disappointing discovery that wherever I go, there I am. Going on a cross-cultural missions adventure will not allow you the luxury of traveling so light that you can store your ego back home in the garage. It tends to travel with you, and will try to trip you up somewhere along the way.

Being at Home in the Place God Puts You

As I read the sixteenth Psalm, I am impressed with the relevance of this Scripture to those of us who struggle with being dislocated from familiar places, and find ourselves in foreign places. In conclusion I'd like to mention three principles that help me to find security in any place God puts me.

1. This space is God's place.

"*Keep me safe, O God, for in you I take refuge,"* David begins.

Safety, security and well being are not exclusive to any geographical location. "*I said to the Lord, you are my Lord, apart from YOU I have no good thing."* Not in this culture or in any other! He is the source of happiness and good. How often, after a particularly abrasive scrape with someone or something in the new place, we start wistfully believing that "back there" in the "good land" it would be different. When things go bad for us in a strange place we need to remind ourselves, *"Lord, you have assigned me my portion and my cup, you have made my lot secure."*

At one time Abraham felt that he had gotten away from God and that he had arrived ahead of God at a certain place. He concluded "*There is surely no fear of God in this place*" (Gen. 20:11), so he took some liberties and let down his moral guard. He asked his wife to lie for him to protect him, because he assumed that the fear of God was not in the place. God is here. His moral control, the fear of Him, has come here ahead of you. This is HIS place. You are not alone. He is here. "*You have made my lot secure."*

In the book *Daybreak over Ecuador* I tried to communicate my admiration for the early missionaries who came. . . and who not only came, but who came to stay. Four of the earliest visitors to Ecuador stayed to serve for over a half century each. They obviously learned the secret of feeling comfortable where they were. And there was no cable TV back then.

Can you imagine what it might have been like? Homer Crisman came in 1897. He left for the last time in 1968, after 71 years of missionary service. He must have been made of other stuff than me, you might say. But he was not. Many times his diary expresses his homesick feelings. There were times when, because of political revolutions, he left his family in the U.S.

Once, while walking at night the ten miles back to his home from the nearest post office, he mulled over a letter he had received that day from his wife. His three year old daughter had apparently been playing with some dolls that would not fit into the toy trunk so her playmate advised, "Just crush it. Just crush it!" A few days later the little girl had come across her mother crying because she had not received a letter from father in some time. Picking up on her friend's advice about the dolls, Homer's daughter walked over to comfort her mom. "Don't cry Mommy, just crush it. It's the only way!"

We often believe that feeling at home in a foreign environment will come to the degree that we are able to surround ourselves with as many of the common and comfortable things of back home as possible . . . Skippy peanut butter, Kellogg's Raisin Bran, VO5 three-in-one shampoo, and Snickers bars in the bottom dresser drawer. Yet we often discover that, despite the things we have around us, that aching need to leave can be triggered by the slightest misfortune . . . an inattentive clerk, a plugged toilet, or a discourteous driver. So what do you do when this character from another culture cooks your tire before your very eyes? What did they teach you in Cross-Cultural Communications 504? What do you do when some little misadventure triggers your desire to travel north, fast? The second principle suggests a solution.

2. God knows I need a safe place.

"You are my hiding place." (Psalm 32:7) The wish to get out of this place can be changed into a quiet resting in God in the place he has put me. Jacob left home, ran away and ended up in a desolate (God-forsaken) place. He slept on a pillow of stone, but there, in his desperate loneliness, the Lord of the universe revealed through a dream that He is present everywhere. And Jacob went on his way KNOWING that, as he put it, *"Surely the Lord is in this place, and I was not aware of it. He was afraid and said ... How awesome is this place!"* (Gen. 28:16,17)

> "The boundary lines have fallen for me in *pleasant places, surely I have a delightful inheritance. I will praise the Lord who counsels me, even at night my heart instructs me. I have set the Lord always before me, Because he is at my right hand I*

> *will not be shaken. Therefore my heart is glad and my tongue rejoices, my body also will rest secure."*
>
> Psalm 16:6-9

It is amazing how safe one can feel when he senses he is in the center of God's will. That still small space in the vortex of strange sounds and unfamiliar food and unusual customs that swirl about you can be the most comfortable spot on the planet. I have never felt safer than in San Francisco de Vergel. I recall lying on a mat on the floor in Carlos Vicente's home after walking two days in the direction of the Amazon river to get there. The lights were out and it was late. Fourteen of us were sleeping in the same room. Seven of us had been total strangers five hours ago. Had something happened to me my wife could not have physically known for at least 48 hours. Yet lying down to sleep in that strange place, I felt strangely safe. You will be safe in the place God sends you, snakes and salamanders and salmonella notwithstanding.

3. God has prepared for me a final place.

It is incredible to discover that many people decide not to go on a short-term missions experience for fear that they may never get back home. They are paralyzed by the fear that something sinister is bound to happen to them "over there" and they will never get back home again. Most of us cross three cultural bridges on our way to coming to stay: The 'I could live here" honeymoon passes with the first hint that 'I could die here', and our immediate reaction is 'get me out of here'. You will usually discover that the Lord orchestrates this significant transition at the worst of moments. The group is getting on the bus to leave for an important ministry engagement when you throw up all over the puppets. You end up staying back in the hotel where you have a whole day by yourself to think about what it would be like to die here, and to wonder if God is really capable of "getting you out of here", or if He even cares.

> *"Because you will not abandon me to the grave, nor will you let your Holy one see decay. You have made known to me the path of life; you will fill me with joy in your presence, with eternal pleasures at your right hand."*
>
> Psalm 16:10-11

The same Jesus who said "*I go to prepare a place for you*," also assured us, *"I am the way, the truth, the life."* I like to think of Him as the route, the reality, and the rest. He is my direction in life and he is my final destination. *"For here we do not have a lasting city . . . but we are seeking the city which is to come."* (Hebrews 13:14) Peter reminds us that wherever we go in this world we will only ever at best be *"aliens and strangers . . ."* anyway! (1 Peter 2:11)

We can go to the most remote region of the world and be totally safe. We can stay at home and suffocate in our pillow. The key is to be found in the place God puts you. Will Mitchell was the missionary who never went. Not because he didn't want to. God had another place for him.

In 1895 at a morning missions conference in Kansas, young people heard about Ecuador, a country closed to evangelical missions. Will Mitchell made a public offer to go as a missionary that morning. He stepped out of the chapel and into a small rowboat to enjoy a moment of relaxation on the lake. He never returned to shore. Yet the "accidental" drowning of Will Mitchell that day was no accident. His comrades returned to the chapel and around the corpse of their friend vowed to take his place. One of them, George Fisher, founded the Gospel Missionary Union and accompanied the first two evangelical missionaries to Ecuador. Will Mitchell fell out of a boat in comfortable Kansas, and died. His two friends faced rock-throwing mobs, yellow fever epidemics, and armed revolutions in hostile Ecuador, but God kept them safe. Will Reed gave more than fifty years of significant service to this country. Homer Crisman was the other.

You don't really suppose
they mean sudden
DEATH playoff, do you?

The truth of the matter is that, if we are walking with Jesus, He will transform any atmosphere and charge any and every place with his Presence, his Peace, and his Power.

> *"Thanks be to God, who always leads us in His triumph in Christ, and manifests through us the sweet aroma of the knowledge of Him in EVERY PLACE."*
>
> 2 Corinthians 2:14

Because of these assuring words we realize that it is truly possible, wherever we are, to be all there. The "I could live here" mode becomes a genuine "I could die here" attitude. He changes the "get me out of here" feeling to gratitude that I can even be here.

To all who face a new experience in some strange new place, may you have the joy of discovering that *"The boundary lines have fallen for me in pleasant places."* A vital relationship with the God of all places, through His Son, Jesus Christ, can alone give you the grace to be happy and useful in any and every place he may happen to put you.

"I thought I told you I was just 'short-term'!"

GETTING STARTED

FULL CONTACT

YOU CAN ONLY BE HAPPY WITH FLOOR EXERCISES for so long. My youngest son Paul loved taekwondo. But it was a large step from floor exercises to full contact. Making the jump to actual combat was not made easier by the fact that he had to do it in another culture and language. But he did. Within seconds his opponent hit him with a well-planted foot to the face. The blood oozed from his nose and he could have quit. But that first shot to the head was like a wake-up call. Paul defended himself well from that moment on, and even scored some points of his own. It was too late to win the match after that first hit, but the battle could still be fought. He went on to outduel his opponent the rest of the way.

Missions is a contact sport. It is time to take that step from floor exercises to full contact. In order for this book to have any practical impact on your life in relation to world missions, you need to get started planning and preparing for a short-term cross-cultural encounter. It does not need to be expensive or exotic. But it does need to have a hands-on feel. That means it will be both traumatic and transformational.

To help you get started this book concludes with a sample survival manual for work teams or summer service missions that has been tried in the trenches of hands-on cross-cultural exposure. You will want to tailor the concept to the details of your particular project. It can be adapted equally well to a trans-cultural experience among native peoples of your own country, or in an inner-city context.

How to Use the Manual

TASKS: The suggested tasks for each day can serve as the guide for a pre-entry orientation study, using the chapters of this manual.

EACH DAY in the field this manual can serve as a journal that will direct you back to one chapter or aspect of cross-cultural dynamics you have read about. That way the lessons will be learned in the crucible of an actual cross cultural context.

HOST: Share this manual with your host missionary or project supervisor so that any changes or corrections can be included in your personalized project journal. Not all of the activities will be applicable or appropriate in the culture you will be visiting.

SURVIVAL SKILLS: The best way to take full advantage of the survival skills in this guide is to make a group pact that each member will help everyone else to complete all of the skills. It will help to build a sense of team spirit among your group, and help the more reluctant types to make contact with the culture.

It's a large step from floor exercises to full contact but you can only be happy with orientation exercises for so long.

Day 1

ORIENTATION

- Cultural Shades: 9:30
- Documents and Dollars
- Scouting About: 10:30

CULTURAL SHADES

Ask a resident of the culture to lead an orientation hour in the special nuances of culture once you arrive in the particular place you will be working. He could use chapter seven as a guide for this session, adapting it to the culture you are visiting. (This does not preclude the importance of having a representative of that culture address your group during pre-trip orientation.)

DOLLARS AND DOCUMENTS

Arrange for photocopies of vital documents such as passports to be deposited in a file folder at the field headquarters, hotel or guest hostel upon arrival. In some countries a photocopy of your passport will be sufficient to travel within the country, so the originals can be kept in a safe central place. Find out what type of currency will be most effective in the country you are visiting, and which form of currency exchange will be the least complicated for your host. Just because you own an impressive array of "good anywhere" credit cards does not mean that people are obliged to accept them. Traveler's checks sound sensible but are sometimes more complicated to exchange than cash or even personal checks.

Plan ahead to do all money exchanging at specific windows in your schedule. There is nothing more demoralizing to a group than to be sitting in a parking lot in a hot bus waiting for Mortimer again because he has "always made it a practice not to cash them till I need them."

SCOUTING ABOUT

Taking a short, guided walking tour to get your feet on the ground and familiarize yourself with the surroundings is helpful when advisable. The more independence you can develop, in the correct sense, the more quickly you will feel safe in your new setting. Your field sponsor needs to advise you on the feasibility of this activity.

Survival Skill # 1: Buy a Coke

Shortly after arrival you need to make your first live transaction in the new currency. The best way to overcome initial stage fright at using the language and the money is to go out and make a purchase.

> *I, ______________________________, hereby certify that ______________________ has successfully passed the basic training test of the purchase of a bottle of Coke, in Spanish, and is herewith authorized to proceed to more advanced cross-cultural training techniques.*

EVENING REFLECTION: Read Acts 7:22-28.

Remember, Moses made some common mistakes in his first transcultural experience we want to watch out for.

- He expected too much
- He acted too quickly
- He quit too soon

WHAT ARE YOUR EXPECTATIONS FOR THIS CROSS-CULTURAL ENCOUNTER?

I expect to ____

____.

I expect to ____

____.

I expect to ____

____.

I expect to ____

____.

FAMOUS FIRST:

Today for the first time I ____

____.

FIRST IMPRESSIONS:

The first thing I noticed about this country and people was ___________

____

____

____

____.

Day 2

BREAKING THE ICE

A short, small-group tour with a national guide to build a bridge across the language barrier.

Survival Skill #2 : First Question Fright

The first time someone asks you a question in Spanish or Swahili is scary. Missionaries never get over the embarrassment of having to ask for things to be repeated, twice. Don't panic! Smile. Say " I don't understand" in the local language. Try to pick up something the second time around. Then panic!

When asked my first question in the language I:

- ❑ smiled and panicked.
- ❑ asked them to repeat it and panicked.
- ❑ answered in English, and then panicked.
- ❑ just plain panicked.

I was able to communicate with _____________ using

- ❑ hand, arm and head signals
- ❑ half English, half Spanish
- ❑ smiles and nods, grunts and groans
- ❑ all of the above

How sorry am I that I didn't spend more time learning more of the language at home?

- ❑ very sorry
- ❑ very, very sorry
- ❑ very, very, very sorry

BONDING Across the Language Barrier

Short-term experiences are successful to the degree that they put people in direct contact with the host culture. Do something early in your trip to deliberately force yourself to bond with the people. This will vary depending on the situation. Sometimes having a meal or even spending a night in the home of a national family is possible. Your resident missionary will know if this is feasible. It may be possible to divide the group into teams of two or three under the guidance of a student who also knows some basic English. These exploratory teams could be given simple assignments such as riding to the end of a bus line and back, visiting a tourist attraction, or attending a home Bible cell. What you do is not as important as whom you do it with.

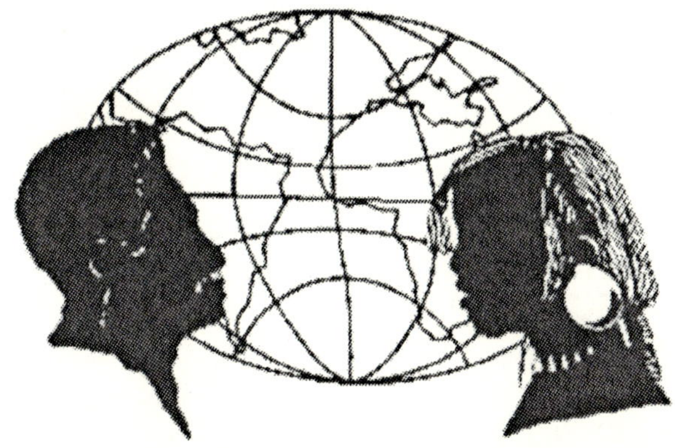

There are many capable, reliable and enthusiastic young people in other cultures who are extremely anxious to relate to people of a second culture. They take the assignment seriously and do the job conscientiously. Entrusting yourself and your total safety to someone of a second culture for an hour or two is an excellent entrance exercise in that culture. We naturally like to be in control of our circumstances. Making genuine contact with another culture is learning that there are some things in my world I will no longer be able to control. Surrendering control of my comfort zone, early in my stay in a new culture, is essential to a happy stay there. If this is done in a safe and "controlled" way it can be a most effective bonding device. It will cause intense anxiety at the outset, but invariably will result in some of the most significant and positive responses to the host culture imaginable.

Day 3

WORK DAY Construction

Survival Skill #3: Other ways to do things

If we are fortunate, we will learn today that there are other ways of doing things. Resist the temptation to want to show them how we do it, or how it should be done. The right way to mix cement is:

A. with a cement mixer.
B. at a ready-mix plant.
C. in a cement truck.
D. the way they did it today.

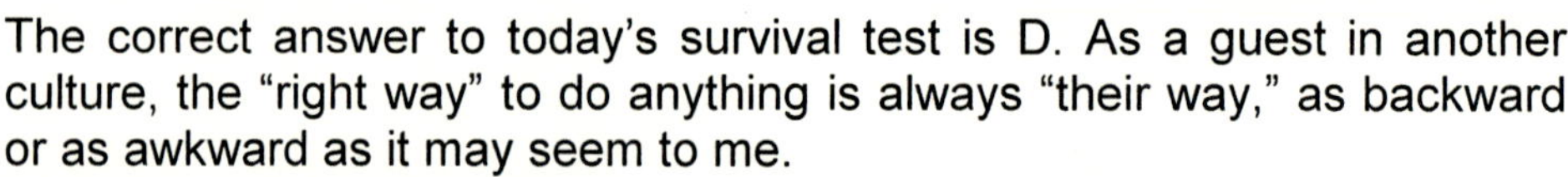

The correct answer to today's survival test is D. As a guest in another culture, the "right way" to do anything is always "their way," as backward or as awkward as it may seem to me.

EVENING REFLECTION:

In chapter ten we read about six practical ways to guarantee a successful short-term experience.

1. Practice low profile, high performance.
2. Be humble about what you have to offer.
3. Be good at what you came to do.
4. Be ready to scrub your plans on arrival.
5. Be modest in your expectation of public ministry.
6. Be balanced in your perception of people's real needs.

Which of these will be hardest to put into practice here, and why?

____

____

Day 4

WORK DAY

- ❑ More church construction
- ❑ Evening guest missionary talk

Survival Skill #4: Copeability

By now you may realize that getting along with people, especially your own people, will move you a long way toward cross-cultural survival. In the end it is not compatibility but copeability that counts. Uneven work assignments, unpredictable team members, unreasonable rules, or just waiting in bathroom lineups, are all ideal indicators of how copeable I really am.

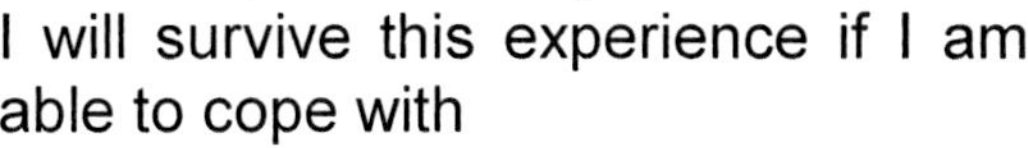

I will survive this experience if I am able to cope with

____

____

___________________________________.

FAMOUS FIRST:

Today for the first time I ______________________________________

Something I have noticed about people here that I like is the way

____.

The first uncomfortable thing that happened to me was when

____

____.

FIRST DEPRESSIONS: CLASSIFYING YOUR DAY

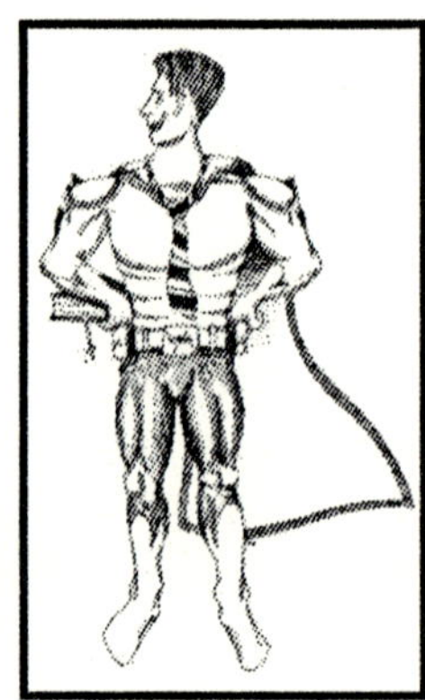

- ❑ Class 1 Day: Today I felt like Wonder Missionary
- ❑ Class 2 Day: I wonder if this is what it really means to be a missionary
- ❑ Class 3 Day: Today I wondered if I have what it takes to be a missionary

WHY? ____

____.

TIME-OUT FOR TEAMMANSHIP

When the sponsors start racing the team members for the hot showers you know it's time for this time out. If the guiding principle of your group is "every man for himself," serious tensions will arise when the normal friction of living and working together is compounded by the cross-cultural factor. Building and maintaining a solid team spirit is essential to a successful experience. Invite a missionary to come in and share, openly, the challenges of working on a team in a cross-cultural environment. Fine tuning your teammanship will be a regular necessity during your time abroad.

DAY 5

WORSHIP IN ANOTHER LANGUAGE

- ❑ Church tour and Worship Service

What things did I notice that they do differently in the church services here?

1. ____
____.
2. ____
____.
3. ____
____.
4. ____
____.

When did I find especially uncomfortable about the way things were done? ____
____.

What did I like most about the way they worshipped... something I wish we did at home?____
____.

I especially sensed the Lord's presence during ______________________
____.

DAY 6

IN-COUNTRY TRAVEL TO...

- ❑ Survival Skill #5: Take a bus trip somewhere
- ❑ Survival Skill #6: Live to tell about it

Survival Skills: Public Transportation

No cross-cultural experience is complete without a trip on public transit. Some key survival rules to consider:

1. My personal space is anything from my skin inward.
   - ➢ The rest of the real estate in the vehicle can and will be occupied. What I do not claim, someone else will.
2. Though I may be in an English-speaking majority, etiquette demands that I speak quietly.
3. The goal of the trip is not just to get there, but to get as many people there as possible.
4. The golden rule of standing in a bus will be observed:
   - ➢ Why squeeze to the back when it feels so good to stand on each other's feet up here at the front?
5. Bladders can and will expand as I journey.

FAMOUS FIRST:

Today for the first time I ____

____

____

____.

DAY 7

A DAY WITH A NATIONAL FAMILY

- Our hosts have assigned us to spend a day in a national home.

Survival Skill #7: Eating With a Smile

We may not like the look of what we eat, and the taste may not do anything to change our opinion, but we don't have to let anyone know how we feel. Put a great big smile on your face and swallow hard. There's more where that came from! If it helps, you are being served the very best your hosts have to offer, prepared in the most careful manner they know how. And you can be sure that someone is watching to see if you like it.

SOMETHING I LIKED about the day: ______________________________
____.

SOMETHING I DISLIKED about the day: ___________________________
____.

WHAT THEY ARE LIKE: ____
____.

WHAT THEY TAUGHT ME: ____
____.

DAY 8

A DAY WITH A MISSIONARY

Team members will be paired with a full-time field missionary to do a task required by that person, to become familiar with him as a person, and to learn about his assignment

Survival Skill #8: Getting under a Missionary's Skin

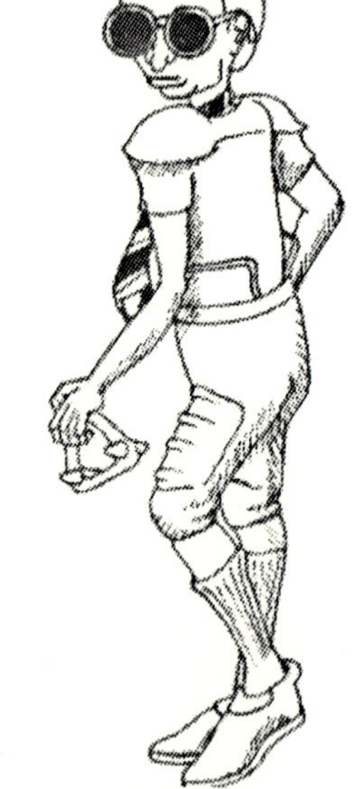

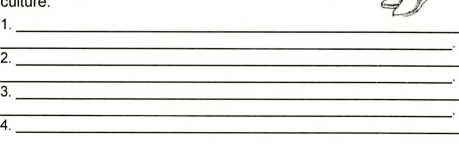

If possible, arrange to have some one-on-one time with one of the resident missionaries. Reread chapter three of the manual so you have some good questions to ask, and know some questions to avoid. The secret of survival today is to get to know a missionary very well and still want to be one.

Questions I'd like to ask a missionary in this culture:

1. ____
____.

2. ____
____.

3. ____
____.

4. ____
____.

The missionary, ______________________________,
responded to my questions this way:

1. ____.
2. ____.
3. ____.
4. ____.

What “sacrifices” do the missionaries I met make in order to be here? ____.

What “mistakes” that Moses made have I detected in some of the people who are working here all the time?

____.

How does this missionary’s heart for the people come through?

____.

DAY 9

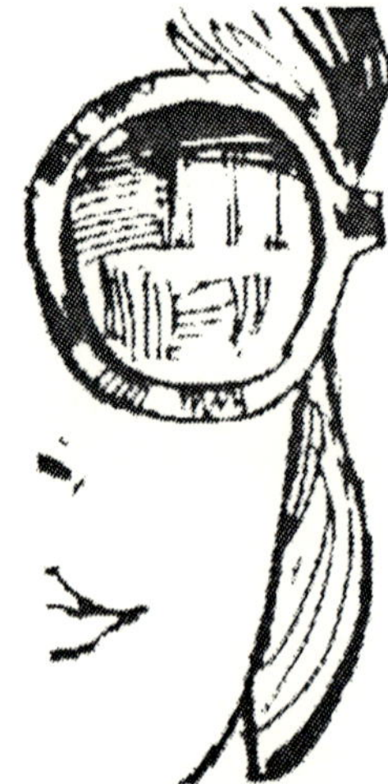

CULTURAL STUDY: OBSERVATION

- ❑ Divide the team in pairs to explore the culture

Practical Tips on What to Look For:

Paul took a walk around Athens and then strolled the streets of Crete. What did he watch for? Here's the checklist from chapter six on how to look at another culture. In order to fulfill today's requirement, I intend to do two of the following exercises suggested in the chapter entitled "How to Look at another Culture":

- ❑ Step inside a hardware store and study the process by which people find clerks, choose items, make purchases and receive their merchandise. Don't be in a hurry!
- ❑ Sit at the back of a bus and ride a complete route observing the following: how to pay, what happens when you don't have the right change, how to stop the bus from inside and outside, how people relate to each other on the bus, what are the attitudes to women, children, the elderly, who gets off where?
- ❑ Stand on a busy street corner or public park for a full two hours and write down everything you see. How the shoe shine boy signals to his clients, etc.
- ❑ Sit in a cathedral for at least an hour and study faces, gestures, and attitudes, counting people, timing their average stay inside, estimating ages, charting their age against their attention span, what did they come for, how did they leave?
- ❑ Ask a resident to point you to a government office where there is heavy paperwork traffic. Sit in the main waiting room and try to figure out the system. Who goes where to get what done? Check out the office of immigration, the transit department, or the social security building.
- ❑ Spend an afternoon wandering the city's transit terminal till you understand the way it works.
- ❑ Watch a policeman at work on a busy corner for an hour.

OBSERVATIONS

My first impression of the scene was ____________________________

____

____.

I began to feel comfortable on the scene after _______________

____

____.

Things I saw after awhile that I had missed at first: ___________

____

____

____

____.

Photo Guidelines and Journal:

- Attempt to get at least one picture that might represent each of the key areas of tomorrow's analysis.
- Don't take pictures of military personnel or policemen without asking permission.

DAY 10

CULTURAL STUDY: ANALYSIS

- Smaller group tours of key institutions such as schools, factories, prisons, markets, malls and government offices.
- Spend an evening swapping discoveries

Finding the answers to the key questions of chapter seven will be hard work. Start early in your visit, and ask as many people as possible about the topics. Choose one or two places to visit and research and spend quality time observing.

1. The food supply and basic services of the country: ____________
____
____
______________________________.

2. The military and police system: ____________________
____
____
______________________________.

3. The spiritual base and resources of the people: ____________
____
____
______________________________.

4. The judicial system: __________________________
____
____
______________________________.

5. The educational system:______________________
____

____

________________________________.

What I most like about this culture: __________________________

____

____.

What I would like to change in this culture: ______________________

____

____.

A personal response to the culture in form of a poem, or a prayer for the people of this place: ______________________________

____

____

____

____

____

____

____

____

_______________________________.

Day 11

Cultural Study: Confrontation

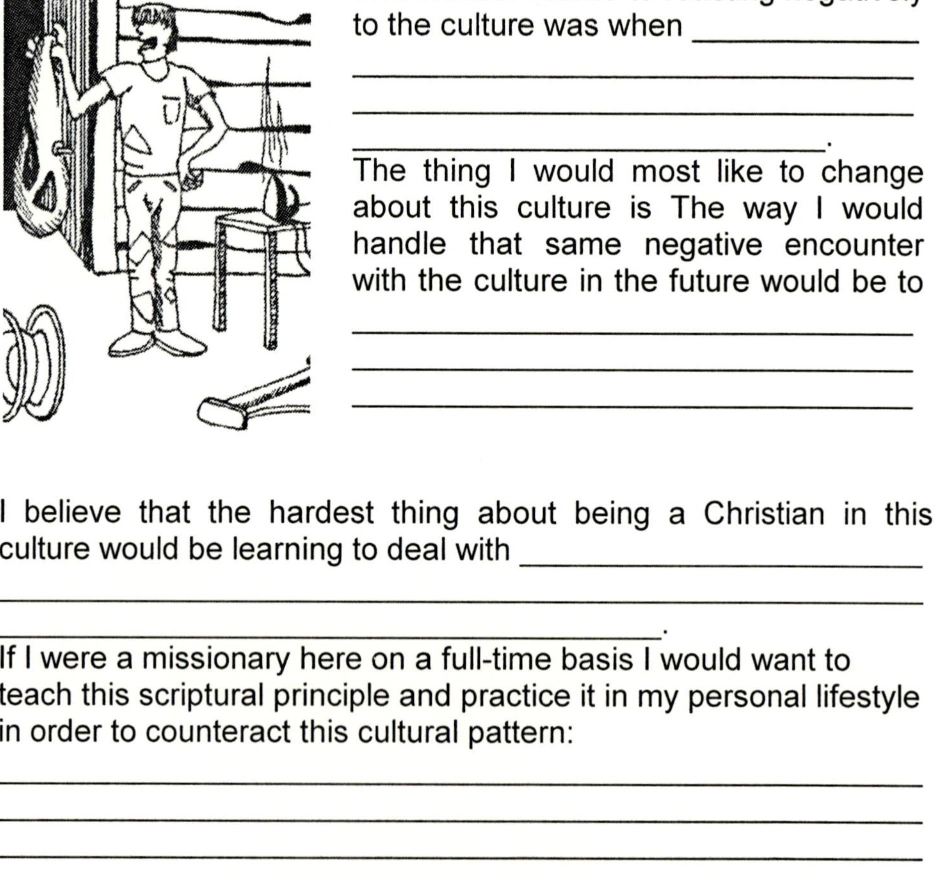

The closest I came to reacting negatively to the culture was when ______________

____

____

______________________________.

The thing I would most like to change about this culture is The way I would handle that same negative encounter with the culture in the future would be to

____

____

____

I believe that the hardest thing about being a Christian in this culture would be learning to deal with ________________________

____

____.

If I were a missionary here on a full-time basis I would want to teach this scriptural principle and practice it in my personal lifestyle in order to counteract this cultural pattern:

____

____

____

___________________________________.

Day 12

MINISTRY

- ❑ Visits to home Bible cells, open air evangelism or film ministry

Survival Skill #9 : Give a testimony through an interpreter

The challenge of ministry in another culture has its own set of rules.
1. To give a testimony that does not rely on cliches that are hard to translate and harder to understand.
2. To sing with enthusiasm even though I don't feel anything.
3. To show interest in the sermon when I don't have a clue what is being said.
4. To adjust my mind, and bottom, to a different time frame.
5. To worship in spirit because I can't yet worship in mind or heart.

FAMOUS FIRST:

Today for the first time I

____

____

____.

My reaction to having had an opportunity to minister to people of another culture:

____

____

____.

Day 13

PACKING FOR HOME!

- Personal DEBRIEFING
- Relax and Reflect

What are you taking back with you besides dirty clothes? souvenirs? battle scars? sad memories?
What am I NOT taking back with me that I had when I came?

1. Something material I lost or gave away:____.

2. Something emotional or attitudinal that I needed to get rid of: ____.

3. Some spiritual contribution I made to someone in our group or someone I met: ____.

4. The first thing I want to do when I get home is: ____.

5. The one thing about my lifestyle I want to change as a result of this trip is: ____.

In chapter twelve we read that the most discouraging experience of cross-cultural exchange is discovering that wherever I go, there I am. This experience has taught me that I still need to let God have control of __________________ because it raised its ugly head on this trip when ____
____
____.

CLOSURE:
Have I said goodbye to some of the significant people I met during the trip?
As we said goodbye to _____________________________ and to ____, I felt as if
____
____

What I want to remember about my time with _______________ is
____
____
____________________________________.

FAMOUS LAST:
Today for the last time I ____
____
____________________________________.

RELAX AND REFLECT:
When you get off that airplane, you will be swept up in a whirlwind of emotion that will make it difficult for you to put together some of the memorable moments of your visit. Take time to do it now.

Most MEMORABLE Moments:
My most unforgettable memory of this trip is _____________________
____
____________________________________.

My most embarrassing moment of this experience was ____.

The most frightening experience of my visit was ____.

The most enjoyable time I had on my trip was ____.

For me, the most frustrating part of living in another culture would probably be ____.

The worst part of this experience was ____.

Day 14

HOMEWARD BOUND

- ❑ In-Flight Self Study

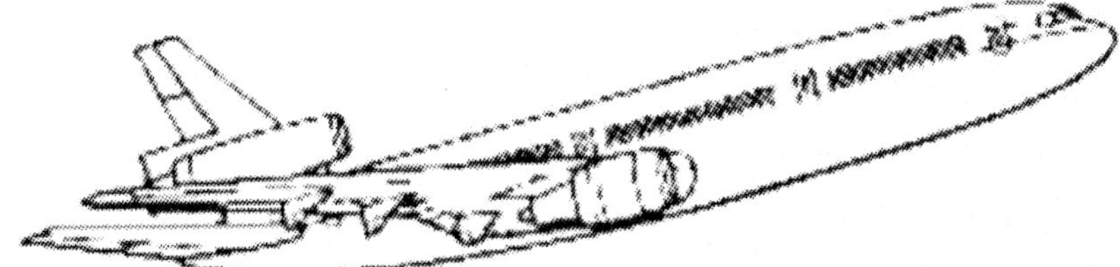

Chapter ten talks about the "waste" being worth it if the goal is great enough. As I analyze my short-term missions experience, I would have to say that one of the biggest extravagances I saw or participated in during my time in the culture was ________________
____
____
____
______________________________________.

My response to the poverty I observed was ____________________
____
____
______________________________________.

In the light of my new insights and awareness of the host culture, I feel that I would recommend/not recommend the experience to others as a worthwhile investment. ________________________
____
____
______________________________________.

Why was the trip worth it? ____________________________________
____
____
______________________________________.

THE TRUST TEST

Chapter five addresses the "The Trust Factor," and mentions four ways God builds our trust in Him. Try to identify what the Lord has taught you about trusting Him in each of the four areas, illustrating it with experiences you had during your stay:

TRUSTING HIM FOR THE LITTLE THINGS:

I learned to trust Him for ______________________ when__________

____

_________________________________.

TRUSTING HIM FOR THE LARGER THINGS:

I learned to trust Him for ___________________________________

______________when_ ____

_________________________________.

TRUSTING HIM WITH THE LOVES OF MY LIFE:

I learned to trust Him with __________________________ and with ________________________________ during this experience and believe that I need to learn to trust Him with ________________

____

____ before I could really serve effectively cross culturally.

TRUSTING HIM WITH MY LIFE ITSELF:

The experience that most made me think that I might never get out of this place alive was ___________________________________

____

____

_________________________________.

Now that I have a little time to sit back and reflect on our experience, I ask myself: "What would it take to get me back here as a missionary?"

I think I could take everything about missionary life except for the

____

____.

From what I have seen, the hardest part of being a missionary would be ____.

____.

The best part of coming back would be _________________________

____

____.

The next time I come on a short-term work assignment, I would pay more attention to ____

____

____.

Printed in the United States
998100004B